That Winning Feeling! Program Your Mind for Peak Performance is all about choosing your future as a rider—and perhaps as a human being.

Jane Savoie presents a revolutionary approach to riding by which you can train your mind and shape your attitudes to achieve higher levels of skill than ever imagined. Psychocybernetics, the science of positive mind power, will show you how to replace your negative perceptions with creative, constructive, and *practical* ideas.

The book deals with such concepts as luck, worry, dreams, "loser's limp," commitment, criticism, frustration, and inspiration. You will learn relaxation exercises that will not only rid you of stress and tension, but will also enable you to benefit fully from the use of "imaging" as a working tool to achieve desired ends. And you will skillfully invoke the "*As if* principle" to think and behave "as if" you are already experiencing your wants and needs.

The author also explains how words, and word-images, play a major role in determining your actions. For instance, if you say "challenge" instead of "problem," you will positively enhance your performance. Conversely, if you speak negatively, you will decrease your chances of success.

The "Training" chapters of the book take all the general principles and apply them to specific riding situations. The book's final chapters deal with "Competition," focusing all the tools and techniques learned earlier on actual performance scenarios.

Throughout the informative and spirited text, there are scores of personal anecdotes about some of America's leading riders — and their affinity with the ideas and teachings of the author.

We all have dreams. How many people are fortunate enough to live them? Jane Savoie not only knows how — but shares all her insights, creativity, and inspiration so that you too can experience the high of *That Winning Feeling!*

Jane Savoie, born and raised in Massachusetts, attended the University of Massachusetts at Amherst and received a B.S. in Animal Science. She rode hunters as a child, evented in college, and began specializing in dressage in 1976 when she moved to Vermont. She ran the riding program at the Vershire School Stables, 1976-80. Since 1980, she has been a freelance dressage instructor, traveling clinician, trainer, and competitor with her home bases in South Strafford, Vermont and Wellington, Florida. She was the reserve rider for the Olympic Team for Barcelona in 1992 and dressage coach for the Canadian Three-Day Event Team at the 1996 Olympics in Atlanta.

The Author on Jolicoeur

That Winning Feeling!

Program Your Mind for Peak Performance

JANE SAVOIE

Drawings by Beth Preston

Foreword by Robert Dover

Trafalgar Square Publishing

NORTH POMFRET, VERMONT

Published in 1992 by
Trafalgar Square Publishing
North Pomfret, Vermont 05053

First published in paperback with a new sub-title and new preface in 1997

Library of Congress Cataloging-in-Publication Data

Savoie, Jane, 1949 –
    That winning feeling! : program your mind for peak performance / Jane Savoie ; drawings by Beth Preston ; foreword by Robert Dover.
        p.   cm.
    Includes bibliographical references (p.   ) and index.
    ISBN 1-57076-049-7 (pbk.)
    1. Horsemanship—Psychological aspects.   I. Title.
SF309.S33   1997
798.2'01'9 — DC21   97-121
                                                                          CIP
ISBN: 1-57076-049-7

Printed in the United States of America
10 9 8 7 6 5 4 3 2

Interior design by Mark Gabor
Cover design by Sally Sherman

Acknowledgments

Of all the pages in this book, this one is the most fun to write. I am pleased to be able to acknowledge the enormous contributions of those who helped turn this dream into a reality.

To my husband, Rhett, whose love and support have been the constant in my life, enabling me to pursue my dreams wholeheartedly.

To my parents, Benjamin Elkind and Lorraine Kaplan, who sometimes believed in me more than I did myself. From as early as I can remember, it was instilled in me that no task was beyond my capabilities.

To all my mentors for their skill and knowledge. To Dr. John McCauley, my sports psychologist, who guided me through much of the material in Part One. To Jane Hamlin, a gifted teacher and trainer, for her expertise with the jumping segments. To my illustrator, Beth Preston, for the imagination and artistry which allowed her to interpret concepts that existed only in my head. To Susan Sexton, who so very generously donated her beautiful photographs simply because she believed in this project. To my editor, Mark Gabor, for his genius and enthusiasm as well as the countless hours spent editing and arranging the book. To my publisher, Caroline Robbins, who took a chance with a first-time author. I have tremendous admiration for her scrupulous attention to detail as well as her enormous patience deciphering my sometimes unclear, wordy "stories."

To my dear friends, Jane Ashley, Susan Blinks, Sally Dininny, Jane Hamlin, Ann Kitchel, Mimi Regamey, and Mary Savidge for their unconditional love, support, and encouragement throughout this and all my other endeavors.

Lastly, to all my students and acquaintances whose affection for their horses motivated me to write such a book in the first place.

Dedicated with love to my husband
Rhett B. Savoie
who taught me how to have
that winning feeling

Preface

It's been several years since *That Winning Feeling!* was first published, and I'm delighted to say that I've heard from lots of readers who have "figured it out." They realized that this isn't just a horse book. It's not about competition; and it's definitely not about ending up in first place on the scoreboard.

Instead, it's a "life" book. It's about struggling and picking yourself back up when you feel like there's nothing left inside of you. It's about doing your best and facing the consequences of your efforts with no excuses. It's about taking the principles described within and courageously applying them to so many other areas of your life — from your career, personal relationships, other sports, as well as to your health.

Surprisingly, many people who train and compete dogs were among the first to write and tell me how they had adapted the concepts in *That Winning Feeling!* to their work. They were excited as they celebrated the joy of communicating with their animals and striving for peak performance.

I'm particularly pleased for those who have used this book to find the strength to deal with the grief of losing a loved one, to actively participate in their own physical healing, and to "soldier on" in spite of all the cards being stacked against them, like the woman who wrote to me after having suffered a severe traumatic brain injury. She could barely talk or control her body, and the doctors gave her little hope; but this determined young woman is now riding again and has set some very lofty goals for herself.

I'm also continually astounded by those who have told me incredible stories about overcoming paralyzing fears — like the woman I met at one of my seminars who had a serious fall from her horse. Her body healed in time, but her mind was much more seriously damaged. Her fears escalated, and in fact, became so overwhelming that even the thought of going into her horse's stall to groom him would fill her with dread and cause her to break into a cold sweat. Eventually, through the use of daily, vivid imaging where she "saw" herself easily coping with her horse in all situations, she soon regained her confidence and once again enjoyed the time she spent with her horse.

I applaud all these people. I continue on my own journey as well. In particular, I have to chuckle when I look back to my college years. Would you believe that I was the person who was so shy that I threatened to drop out rather than give a fifteen-minute talk in front of thirty people in a required speech class? Now I travel all over the country giving motivational speeches to large groups, and if you want me to stop talking, you have to pry the microphone out of my hand!

And, of course, I continue to learn on a daily basis from my students and the horses I meet. They teach me lessons about respect, communication, patience, self-discipline, and introspection.

So, to all my old friends I say, keep up the great work. For those of you about to embark on this adventure, my wish is for you to squeeze every last drop out of this book. Use it for the inspiration as well as the information that will help you to capture "that winning feeling."

If you can dream it, you can do it.

—J.E.S. 1997

Preface to the First Edition

During a training session at the United States Equestrian Team (USET) headquarters in Gladstone, New Jersey in 1976, I observed the United States' top dressage riders and their coach, Colonel Bengt Ljungquist, at work. I was so inspired by their dedication and the beauty of the partnership between horse and rider that I decided, "This is what I want to do."

I was poorly equipped to undertake this quest. I did not own a horse, had very limited finances, was of average ability, and had minimal experience. Yet sixteen years later I have represented the United States at the North American Championships in Canada, have had three horses named to the United States Equestrian Team long lists, have qualified for three United States Olympic Festivals, have won many Horse of the Year Awards, and was given a major grant by the USET to train and compete in Europe in preparation for the 1992 Olympic Games.

My limitations might be reminiscent of your situation. What, then, has made the difference for me?—Attitude and Mental Training.

I am not a trained psychologist and therefore probably have no business writing a book embracing psychological principles. But I've repeatedly used the techniques described in this book to overcome my personal obstacles. They have worked for me, and although they might not all apply to your particular problems, perhaps some of them will enhance your training and performance.

In addition, once you develop the right attitude and master skills such as imaging and relaxation, you'll find that their application goes far beyond the stable. So—under the guise of a horse book—I happily offer you concepts and methods to enrich other aspects of your life.

—J.E.S.

Foreword

When Jane Savoie asked me to write a foreword to her book, *That Winning Feeling!*, I must admit that I had my doubts. Another riding manual, another how-to book for aspiring dressage riders, I thought. How wrong I was! I should have known that nothing so mundane could ever come out of "my Jane Savoie." I would like to state categorically that I was totally overjoyed by reading *That Winning Feeling!* Not only is it wonderfully written but it encompasses a philosophy through which riders (nay, all people) may learn to advance themselves toward whatever their goal might be.

Jane Savoie has not merely written this book; she has lived it. I first met Jane in 1980 in the Boston area where I was instructing. I immediately recognized that she had something that went far beyond sheer talent — a kind of focus that took every situation and made the best of it. Jane's was far less than the perfect scenario: she had one horse schooling in the higher levels which, owing to soundness problems, had developed some difficult evasions. That, however, did not stop her, and over time Jane patiently and lovingly taught her horse all the Grand Prix lessons. She has since then gone on to train many horses for herself and others — and was the reserve rider for the 1992 bronze medal dressage team at the Olympics in Barcelona.

From an outsider's point of view, Jane Savoie has certainly not had an easy time of it. She was not born into wealth; she has not been blessed, up until recently, with the greatest of horses; and she has taken, as we all have from time to time, the wrong paths. But Jane is an expert survivor, and the secrets of her great will and ongoing love of dressage are now available for all to read. If you are not a horseperson, just plug in any other sport, hobby, or endeavor in place of riding — and all of the rewards of this book will be there for the taking.

That Winning Feeling! is a testament to wonderful a person who would love nothing greater than to help all of us others to excel as she has. I personally plan to use the theories in Jane's book to advance myself and my students in our art and sport. I hope that all of you will do the same.

—Robert Dover, *Four-time Olympian*

Contents

Acknowledgments

Preface

Foreword by Robert Dover

Introduction

PART ONE: ATTITUDE AND MENTAL TRAINING

1 WIN with Psychocybernetics   2
The WIN Mechanism   2
  ● *Goals*   5
  ● *Negative Goals*   7
  ● *Luck*   9
  ● *Dreams*   10
  ● *Work*   11
  ● *Commitment*   11
  ● *Persistence*   12
  ● *Belief*   12
Imaginary Experience   15
Mental Images   18
  ● *Relaxation Exercises*   18
  ● *Exercises to Enhance Visualization Skills*   22
  ● *Get Emotionally Involved*   27
  ● *Conclusion*   27

2 WIN with Words   28
What You Say *Is* What you Get   28
Censor Your Speech   31
Positive Self-Talk   35
Capture the Power of Words   36

3 WIN with the As If Principle 38

Psychocybernetics and the As If Principle 38
Using the As If Principle to Handle Show-Nerves 39
Assuming Desirable Qualities 40
- *Enthusiasm* 40
- *Courage* 41
- *Patience* 43
- *Poise* 44
- *Confidence* 44
- *Discipline* 45

4 Positively Riding 46

- *Attitude* 46
- *Self-Image* 48
- *Cancel the Negative* 48
- *Thought-Stopping* 51
- *Worry* 52
- *Sources of Inspiration* 54
- *Criticism* 54
- *Loser's Limp* 56

PART TWO: TRAINING

5 Behavior Modification 68

The Stimulus 69
- *Consistency of Aids* 69
- *Analyzing Movements* 72
Reinforcement 73
- *Reward* 73
- *Punishment* 74
One Practical Application of Behavior Modification 79

6 Applying Your WIN Mechanism 82

Using Psychocybernetics 82
Applying the Power of Positive Speech 85
Incorporating the As If Principle in Training 86

7 *The Positive Approach to Training Challenges*   87
Resistance   87
Emotional Control   94
  • *Frustration*   94
  • *Your Mental View*   96
  • *Your Nature*   100
Physical Control   101
Positive Mental Training   104

PART THREE: COMPETITION

8 *Preparation*   111
The Dressage Test   111
Memorizing Dressage Tests and Jumping Courses   116
Further Use of Psychocybernetics in Competition   120
Rehearsal   123
Reducing Tension   125

9 *It's Showtime!*   127
Arrive Early   127
Observe Other Riders   129
Warm-Up   130

10 *Attitude*   133
Develop a Winning Attitude   133
Show-Nerves   134
Stay Positive   137
Winning and Losing   138

Footnotes   142
Photo Credits   143
Index   144

Introduction

Riding, training, and competing are primarily functions of the body. Riding, training, and competing *successfully* are primarily functions of the mind. If you are reasonably athletic and coordinated, you can become a competent rider. What separates the good rider from the great rider is what goes on in the mind.

Too often a gifted rider never rises above mediocrity. It's convenient to blame things such as bad luck, bad timing, or limited finances. Few would dispute that such obstacles can be overwhelming. These very real excuses, however, are not in your own best interests. You can take the first step toward commanding your future by regarding your attitude and lack of mental training as the major causes of your failure to reach your goals. If you control your thinking, you can begin to control your life.

"Al Oerter, an athlete whose career in discus throwing spans two decades of competition for Olympic gold, sums up the relative importance of attitude. He claims that by the time he learned how to use his mental skills as an athlete, he realized success was 90% mental, 10% skill — 90% the way he looked at it, 10% what he had going in."[1]

You know that you love your horse. But there are times you'd like to quit and take up bowling! Don't. Instead, prepare yourself for an exciting equestrian adventure. With the right attitude and mental training, you alone will determine the degree of fun and success you can have with your horse. No longer will you feel controlled by your horse's behavior or other external circumstances. You might not be able to change what happens to you, but you alone decide how you'll react to those situations. Think of yourself and your horse as a living laboratory. Enjoy the experiments and the process of "becoming." All you have to lose is frustration and tension.

Your adventure starts with an open-mindedness that will enable you to reach your training, riding, and competitive goals through an understanding of the human mind and how one facet of it operates. You will discover the powerful WIN mechanism you have within you that when properly programmed can deliver whatever you desire. You will learn how to WIN by controlling your imagination, your speech, and your actions.

To Win — let us understand — is not necessarily limited to bringing home the blue ribbon. It is developing your potential and using it for a purpose that makes you happy. It is leaving your all-too-familiar comfort zone and striving for more than you thought you could achieve. It is putting forth the kind of effort that makes you proud to sign your name to your work. Winning is doing your personal best.

Part One

ATTITUDE AND MENTAL TRAINING

Attitude, not aptitude, determines altitude
— Z. Ziglar

1

WIN *with Psychocybernetics*

Have you ever said, "I wish I could relax at competitions" or "I wish I didn't feel insecure competing against the professionals or riding for important judges" or "I wish I could coordinate my body when asking for a shoulder-in?" Well, guess what? You can get your wish! Through the application of psychocybernetic principles, you have the necessary tools to accomplish whatever you like. You can choose your future.

Dr. Maxwell Maltz, world-renowned plastic surgeon and author of *Psycho-Cybernetics*, coined the word "psycho-cybernetics" to describe the principles of cybernetics (the goal-striving behavior of machines and mechanical systems) as applied to human beings. According to Maltz, the subconscious mind functions in the following ways:

- It consists, in part, of a goal-striving mechanism that seeks to accomplish the pictures created in our imagination
- It can not tell the difference between what is real and what is imagined
- It needs images to be vivid in order to work most efficiently

The WIN Mechanism

The subconscious mind is that part of the mind which is "not wholly conscious, but capable of being made conscious."[2] It consists, in part, of a goal-striving mechanism that is impersonal and nonjudgmental. It will do its best to accomplish whatever clear-cut goal you put in front of it. It does not care if the goal is positive or negative (success or failure). Whatever the goal, it will do its best to carry it out.

In other words, you can say to yourself at any time, "I can achieve **Whatever I Need, and WIN**." This word-message is useful to have in your mind at all times. For this reason I will use the letters WIN throughout the book to indicate the *mental functions that produce the positive benefits of your goal-striving mechanism.*

You alone decide whether you will program your subconscious mind as a WIN mechanism or as a LOSE mechanism. For instance, if you repeatedly say, think, and picture your horse refusing ditches, shying at the judge's stand, or stiffening in canter departs—then he will (fig. 1). Your body reacts in a way that helps you achieve whatever goal the mind thinks you desire. On the other hand, if you begin to imagine you and your horse confidently and happily jumping ditches, trotting by the judges stand, and doing fluid canter transitions, your mind will enable you to turn what you imagine into reality.

1   *If you repeatedly say, think, and picture your horse shying at the judge's stand—then he will*

According to Dr. Maltz, the goals that the mind seeks are mental pictures created by our imagination. It is irrelevant that the goals might seem out of reach and the means to your desired end are not apparent. If you can vividly imagine your goal *as already in existence*, your WIN mechanism will supply the means.

Take, for example, my experience at the screening trials for the North American Championships, a dressage competition held between the United States and Canada. In 1989, it was held at Windedge Farm in St. Justin de Newton in Canada. I had a whole bunch of facts that supported the improbability of my doing well at the screening trials. I did have a top horse, Zapatero, to compete. But the other facts were:

- Zapatero was new to me, and we had not had time to develop a solid relationship and real communication
- He was a young horse and not yet strong enough to do what was required
- Although confident at the Prix St. Georges level, we were not comfortable with the requirements at Intermediare 1 (full pirouettes, zigzags in trot and canter, flying changes of lead every second stride)

These facts made it difficult to imagine the perfect test. So I visualized the awards ceremony instead. Several times over the course of the day, I would find a quiet spot, close my eyes, relax, and visualize leading the victory lap (fig. 2). In the process, I stopped thinking about the "facts" and thus prevented doubts and insecurities from creeping in. Later, when the results were posted, Zapatero and I were, in fact, there to lead the lap of honor.

It sounds incredible, and I in no way minimize the necessity for all the preparation and hard work involved. But mentally zeroing in on desired results as if they were already in existence was a significant factor in our ultimate success. It was important to focus on a positive outcome as a foregone conclusion rather than allow my rather vivid imagination to conjure up failure pictures. My mind could then supply the means to achieve my goal by helping me to ride skillfully and effectively.

Goals

Your WIN mechanism must have a clear-cut objective to work on, so setting specific goals is vital to your success. "If you fail to plan, then you plan to fail."[3] Establish long-term goals (yearly and for your career) as well as short-term goals (daily, weekly, monthly).

Let's say that your long-term goal for the coming year is to qualify your Training Level horse for the National Dressage Championships at First Level. Find out the date and place of these championships. Write them on a card, e.g., " September 16-18, Lexington, Virginia." Then post that card on your tack trunk or refrigerator or some other place where you'll see it often. Even when you are not consciously reading the card, your mind will absorb it and eventually accept it as its mission.

2   *Find a quiet spot, close your eyes, relax, and*
visualize leading the victory lap

Set aside some time each day to visualize your goal. See yourself pulling onto the showgrounds, locating your stall, and settling your horse in (fig. 3). Savor the excitement of having earned the right to compete. Make a mind's-eye movie of all the details of your experiences (see pp. 16 and 119). Picture your goal as already in existence, and you'll be well on your way to achieving it.

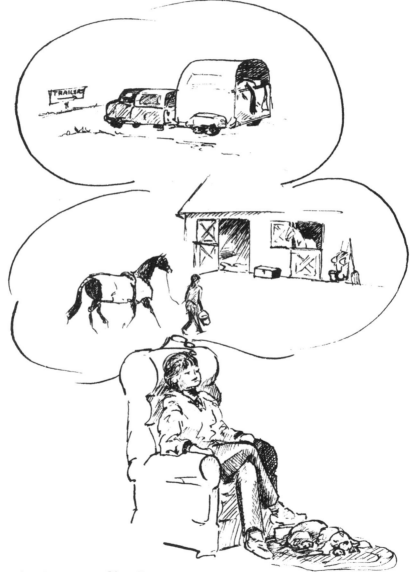

3   *See yourself pulling into the showgrounds, locating your*
stall, and settling your horse in

To bring yourself step-by-step closer to your long-term goal, set up specific short-term goals. Devise a plan, and as you concentrate on each stage, don't worry about the next phase until the time comes.

Part of having goals is to prepare yourself to deal with the inevitable setbacks that occur. When you encounter a setback, make a new set of goals quickly. Don't completely abandon your original goal. Just make a temporary alternate plan. Otherwise, your setback will be frustrating because you'll have set a goal that you are unable to attain.

So when one door closes, look for other options. Rather than feeling defeated, develop an attitude that will allow disappointments to hold the possibility of comparable or better opportunities. Let's say that during your preparations to compete in the season's first show, your horse comes up with a tendon problem. While he heals, set a new goal. Use your newly available time to educate yourself through auditing clinics and attending forums or to make more money to put aside for a new horse or for future training.

Setbacks need not overwhelm you. Just be flexible enough to consider alternate plans until you can get back to your original goal or an even better one.

Negative Goals

Your WIN mechanism's only purpose is to help you achieve your goal. It is like a guided missile. It gets a fix on its target — but if you shift your objective it will make whatever corrections are necessary to accomplish its mission. So be very careful what you vividly *pre*create in your imagination because sooner or later your mind will make it come to pass.

Take, for example, the extraordinary story of the man working on a railroad in Russia. He accidentally locked himself into a refrigerator car. Panic set in. He banged on the door and screamed, but no one heard him. Finally, he accepted the inevitable and prepared to die. He scribbled a message on the wall: "I'm becoming colder now. Starting to shiver. Nothing to do but wait. I am slowly freezing to death. Half asleep now. I can hardly write. These may be my last words."

They were. Five hours later, the door was opened and he was found dead.

Incredibly, the temperature in the car was 56 degrees. The refrigeration unit had been broken, and there was plenty of oxygen. The man essentially willed himself to die. He vividly imagined he would freeze to death — and he did.[4]

Since your WIN mechanism never rests, it's vital to acknowledge the inevitable outcome of the pictures you see in your mind's eye. If your images are undesirable, unfortunate things are bound to happen. "Your mind will bring you what you want or don't want according to the instructions you give it."[5]

When you visualize yourself going over a jump, your subconscious tries to fulfill your mental picture. Visualize wiping out and the subconscious cheerfully responds, "Here's a wipe-out!" If you want to get your subconscious really confused, according to Robert Rotella, director of sport psychology at the University of Virginia and consultant to the United States Equestrian Team, think about not wanting to land in the water before you get to a water jump. Then chew yourself out when the water is where you end up. Your subconscious will say, "You told me water. I give you water and you give me grief about it. I wish you'd make up your mind!" [6] (fig. 4)

Having personally experienced the results of my subconscious mind working hard to help me achieve negative goals, I learned the hard way to recognize and censor negative images before my WIN mechanism became a LOSE mechanism by efficiently carrying out what it thought I desired.

For example, recently I heard that my friend Sandy had broken her collarbone while riding her young mare. The mare hadn't done anything wrong. She had just been typically baby-horse klutzy. She stumbled, fell, and Sandy hit the ground. The following day I was riding Genaldon. I had been working this horse for four years without a mishap. During the warm-up, I was thinking about Sandy and her accident. The next thing I knew, Genaldon fell and skidded several feet on his knees with his nose buried in the dirt. Coincidence? Unlikely. Somehow my mind allowed me to ride him in such a way (perhaps too long, too low, and not paying attention) that it set us up for a fall.

Or consider the time my friends and I were sitting around at lunch discussing our old injuries. I had been kicked a couple of times in the stomach and leg. I'd never been kicked in the face, and the idea so horrified me that I declared I could only imagine how awful the pain would be. Within one hour of that conversation, I was kicked by a loose horse who managed to knock out most of my front teeth and break my upper jaw! How can I explain it? Mere coincidence? I don't believe so. I *do* know that being kicked in the face had just been vividly on my mind.

Luck

Much of what you perceive as good luck or bad luck is the result of your mind striving to reach your goals. The WIN mechanism is so good at its job that it has an almost magnetic attraction. It brings to you whatever you need to realize your goals. Alas, rather than getting the credit it deserves, the work of the mind is too-often passed off as luck.

Through self-awareness and a little practice, you can recognize and take advantage of any opportunities that come your way. The best definition of luck I ever heard is that luck is when opportunity and preparedness meet. "Opportunities are always there. But only people who are prepared get them. If you are prepared, you are lucky. If you are not prepared, you are unlucky."[7]

4 *"You told me water. I give you water, and you give me grief about it!"*

Dreams

Since part of the mind functions as a goal-striving mechanism, it is important to distinguish between goals and wishes. Simply wishing for things you would like is not enough to make it happen. I wish I had a better horse. I wish I could move my horse up to second level. I wish I could win this event. Wishes are the first step, but they need to be substantiated with work.

Your wish is a dream. It is important to dream, for once you stop dreaming you're a goner. It is a sad epitaph that reads, "Dead at 30 . . . . buried at 65." Sometimes our ability to dream gets stifled. Self-doubts, day-to-day survival, and discouragement from significant others inhibit dreams. When that happens, you need to take deliberate steps to encourage yourself to dream again.

How can you do that? Talk to a dreamer and get caught up in the excitement. Sit on a fabulous horse and dream about having a horse of such quality to ride. Go to the big shows. Watch the great riders and dare to think . . . That could be me. Then take comfort in the idea that you would not be given the dream without the capacity to achieve it. Your mind will see to it.

If you are going to dream, you might as well dream big. "Make no little plans. They have no magic to stir your blood."[8] It is hard to get too excited over dreaming about having a new saddle. But how about breaking that saddle in during the National Horse Show?

Some people do not dare to dream big because they don't want to deal with disappointment. Their logic says: if I don't expect to win, I won't be disappointed if I lose . . . . And if I do win, it'll be a bonus.

You don't need to protect yourself like that. In fact, that kind of protection backfires. If you don't expect to win, you probably won't. Occasionally you'll win in spite of yourself or because your "nothing to lose" attitude allows you to remain relaxed. But imagine how many more times you might have been successful if you had bravely decided to win. Drop your protective armor. Commit yourself to your goal. And work diligently towards that end.

Dreaming big is vital, but dreams must also be realistic. Lofty dreams that demand that you stretch yourself are okay. But you must distinguish between big dreams and unrealistic ones. An unrealistic dream, for instance, would be to expect to make the Olympic team this year when you don't know your diagonals yet. A big dream would be to strive to make that team sometime during your lifetime.

Work

Begin with a dream, and then systematically turn that dream into a goal through work. It is important to work hard but just as important to work smart. You have worked hard if you come home from the barn exhausted because you have ridden two horses, mucked several stalls, cleaned tack, stacked hay, and single-handedly emptied the shavings truck. But if your goal is to prepare for a combined training event, working smart might involve hiring someone to clean, lift, and tote while you ride a third horse, run several miles, watch a training session, and find a quiet spot to sit down and visualize your goal.

Work is essential to your success. It is not always the talented rider who excels. Innate ability is important. But the rider of lesser talent who plugs away diligently will inevitably surpass the talented rider who lacks commitment and dedication.

Commitment

An important aspect of work is a willingness to "do whatever it takes." That commitment can make the difference between moderate and substantial success. Do you need to forego some luxuries or take out a loan so you can afford to train with the best professionals? Do you need to undertake a serious fitness program that includes weight training as well as aerobic exercise so you can ride at your optimum? Do you need to schedule daily riding time so that you school your horse consistently, not just when it is convenient? Or maybe you need to spend a couple of months on the longe line to develop your seat.

Perhaps your goal is to create art by performing a moving musical freestyle with your horse. You have fabulous music. You've worked rigorously on the choreography. You've perfected the technical aspects of the movements through conscientious daily schooling. Yet, something is not quite right. How can you create an aesthetically pleasing picture when you are twenty pounds overweight? In this case, commitment to your goal demands that you lose that excess weight.

Depending on your personal challenge, doing whatever is necessary to realize your goal can assume varied and not always pleasant forms. But the depth of your commitment is often the difference between success and failure.

Persistence

So you have a dream and you are willing to work. What other qualities are necessary for success? Persistence is paramount. Dressage rider Robert Dover, veteran of Olympic Games, World Cup, and World Championships, recognizes the absolute necessity of persistence. Robert went to Europe in 1987. He planned to stay eighteen months and gain some international exposure and experience. When he started to compete, he was consistently at the bottom of the pack. In Robert's words, he was "beginning to turn losing into an art form." But he stuck with it. He kept getting himself out there, and he ended up becoming the first American to win the Kur (musical freestyle) at Aachen in almost 30 years. Robert had a dream. He was willing to work. And he persisted in spite of repeated failures.

President Calvin Coolidge once wrote, "Nothing in the world can take the place of persistence. Talent will not. Nothing is more common than unsuccessful men with talent. Genius will not. Unrewarded genius is almost a proverb. Education will not. The world is full of educated derelicts. Persistence, determination, and hard work makes the difference."

Belief

Belief is another quality you must possess to realize your dream. Believe with a kind of blind faith. Believe in yourself and believe in your horse. After all, if you do not believe in yourself, who will? And if you believe, that confidence inevitably shines through.

Take, for example, my experiences at the Palm Beach Dressage Derby in 1989. The Derby was the largest and most prestigious show on the Florida circuit at that time. In 1989 it was designated as a selection trial for the North American Championships, an international dressage competition to be held in Canada the following September.

At the time I was competing two horses. Genaldon was competing at Fourth Level. We had been together since 1985 when he was three-and-a-half years old, and we had a special relationship. I warmed up for classes thinking, feeling, saying, and *believing*, "We're 100% confident . . . 100% confident." We were, and as a result won the majority of our classes.

However, the situation with Zapatero was a bit different. He was entered in the Prix St. Georges as part of the screening trials, and this was only our second time competing together at that level. Saying I was 100% confident was not something I could chant to myself and believe. It was imperative to find something I could believe with the same conviction as with Genaldon.

What I did believe was that he was a super horse with tremendous talent. My refrain became, "You're the best horse here. There are hundreds of horses on these showgrounds, and you're the best." I could believe that wholeheartedly and, therefore, I was able to ride with confidence. As a result we ended up third out of 68 horses and were well on our way to representing the United States at the North American Championships.

Kelli McMullen Temple is fast becoming one of the United States' top Three Day Event riders. In 1989 her horse Macavity was named United States Combined Training Association (USCTA) Horse of the Year, and in 1990 they were long-listed for the World Championships. Along the way to her successes, Kelli learned a hard lesson about believing in herself: Believing is a full-time job.

" . . . the ribbons are the icing on the cake. It's the day-to-day training that I love " — Kelli McMullen Temple

Her horse, nicknamed Max, was a bold, athletic jumper, so cross-country and stadium did not present a particular problem for them. Dressage was a different story. Max had come to Kelli without very good basics. He was extremely crooked and tended to be short, tight, and high in his neck. He had been ridden with harsh bits and crammed into a frame from front to back. As a result they spent a lot of their first year together running around the arena out of control.

But Kelli had faith in her horse. She knew he had tremendous talent and athletic ability and that it was worth putting the time and effort into re-educating him. They went back to basics, and day by day Max's flatwork improved. Plus they developed a rapport that allowed her to ride him with brilliance and still control his exuberant nature.

By the time the Radnor Three Day Event (one of their first major competitions) rolled around, Kelli's belief in herself and her horse had grown so that she was mentally prepared for dressage. She said, "I rode my dressage test so positively and confidently. I felt . . . just wait till they see this horse go." Her attitude enabled her to win the dressage phase over seasoned competitors who were often riding more experienced horses. During the second phase of the event, the cross-country, they went clean and retained their lead.

As she rode into stadium, the third phase of the event, the pressure was on. Here was a relative newcomer challenging the stars of the eventing world. As she thought about the situation, her belief faltered. Kelli said, "All of a sudden I doubted myself. I thought, 'Who am I to be here?' And in those moments of wavering confidence, I lost concentration and pulled a rail. It was the kind of technical mistake I would have made two years ago." That mistake cost her the event, and they dropped to fourth place. Believing in yourself all the time was a tough lesson to learn, but one that made a lasting impression on Kelli.

As Kelli discovered, your conscious mind, with its doubts and insecurities, can undermine your belief. The conscious mind will ask perfectly reasonable questions like:

- What makes you think you can do that?
- Don't you know your horse is not as fancy as the others you are competing against?
- Don't you realize you are an amateur competing against professionals?

You must learn to ignore this interference from your conscious mind and put your trust in the workings of your WIN mechanism.

Imaginary Experience

"Experimental and clinical psychologists have proved beyond a shadow of a doubt that the human nervous system can not tell the difference between an actual experience and an experience imagined vividly and in detail."[9] How wonderful! This means you can use imaginary experience to improve performance. By repeatedly picturing what you desire, your mind believes that you have really done it. In actuality, you may have ridden 20 lousy canter departs on your horse, but since you have mentally practiced 200 lovely departs, your transitions will improve. Practice makes perfect. Since in your mind you have "ridden" ten times more good departs than bad, you begin to actually ride them better because you have more experience doing them that way.

Take, for example, the story of Major Nesmeth, a prisoner of war in North Vietnam. For seven long years he had been confined in a small cage. During that time he kept his sanity by the daily playing of an imaginary eighteen holes of golf. He vividly performed every swing and shot. After his release seven years later, he started playing golf again and found he had shaved 20 points off his old average score! As far as his mind was concerned, he had actually played all those games. He had spent seven years practicing, refining, and perfecting his technique.[10]

Reader's Digest tells of a month-long experiment with three groups of similarly-skilled high school basketball players. Group 1 did not practice and their performance deteriorated. Group 2 practiced one hour per day, and their performance improved by 2%. Group 3 practiced only in their imagination, and their performance improved by 3½%. Group 3 improved the most because when you practice in your imagination, you never miss! [11]

This study shows that performance can be improved by practicing solely in the imagination. Think what this concept can mean to you. Since experiencing something in your mind can be considered in many ways to be the same as experiencing something in actuality, you can in fact become a better rider in the comfort of your own living room. You might only have one horse to ride and limited time, but you can get in many extra hours of quality training in your mind.

Practicing in your imagination has many advantages. Mentally, you can rehearse without pressure because there is nothing to lose. Also, when you practice in your imagination, you never fail. Every shoulder-in is perfect—just the right bend, angle, and balance. If mere physical repetition were the way to improve, you'd be getting worse because you've probably been doing shoulder-ins that are already imperfect.

An Exercise—

Pick a riding problem that has plagued you. Every day find a quiet spot, relax, and visualize in detail you and your horse working through this problem with a successful resolution. *See* the desired end result. Picture yourself sitting correctly and reacting to your horse appropriately. If the image eludes you, watch a very good horse and rider. If you don't have the opportunity to observe accomplished riders at your barn or at shows, watch a video. Capture the scene in your mind's eye, and then see it over and over. Each time, fill in more details. Be sure to practice only when you are relaxed—such as just before you drift off to sleep or just upon awakening. Or practice the relaxation skills offered on p. 18 so you can rehearse at any time of the day. Go through the whole process at least once a day for several weeks. Reserve judgment about whether or not it is working during this period. Draw your conclusion at the end of the several weeks.

For example, let's say you have had a problem with riding downhill to a fence. Imagine smoothly putting your horse in balance before the hill and then shifting your upper body back and dropping your weight down into your heels. You take and give softly on the reins as your horse canters quietly down the hill. *See* the horse jumping the fence, landing smoothly, and galloping off relaxed and in balance. You've kept your weight in your heels and your body is neither too far forward nor too far back.

Now fill in the details. What color is your horse? Are you wearing gloves? Is the ground hard, uneven, or muddy? What is the weather like? Are you alone or riding in company? Experience a sense of calmness and confidence. Enjoy the sensation of your body feeling strong and in control, yet relaxed.

Paint a vivid mental picture and repeat this scenario daily while in a state of deep relaxation.

Perhaps your problem is that your horse consistently shies in the far right corner of the arena (fig. 5). Imagine riding smoothly through that corner. Your horse bends easily, and you enter and leave the corner in perfect balance. You even start to look forward to riding through that corner as an opportunity to rebalance your horse and prepare for the next movement. Your horse is relaxed and listening so attentively to you that he is not distracted by his surroundings. Since he is no longer shying, you don't stiffen. Your breathing remains deep and regular, and your body stays relaxed. Since you are riding a living creature that mirrors what you do and feel, he will be in harmony or discord with whatever you choose. So break the cycle of tension and shying by practicing in your mind.

5   *Perhaps your horse consistently shies in the
far right corner of the arena . . . .*

. . . Imagine riding smoothly through that corner

Mental Images

Significant behavioral and physiological changes occur in those who can experience *vivid* images, but not in those who only experience weak images. Creating vivid images, however, is a skill that can be developed. If you are having difficulty filling in the details, here are some ways to improve your "imaging," as I like to call it. It will take approximately three-to-four months of daily practicing for a 20 minute period to advance from weak to highly detailed images. Do these exercises lying down as opposed to sitting or standing.

Relaxation Exercises

Relaxation is the most important prerequisite for successful imaging. During relaxation your images can become the sole focus of attention. Three types of relaxation exercises are helpful:

a. Diaphragmatic Breathing
b. Progressive Relaxation
c. Autogenic Relaxation

a. The first and simplest relaxation exercise is to practice *diaphragmatic breathing* — also known as *deep breathing*. It might seem odd to have to practice breathing. It's a function we do involuntarily and automatically to survive. When tense, however, we breathe shallowly and often even hold our breath. We can break the cycle of tension by consciously breathing smoothly and deeply.

Watch a dog or cat breathe while it is resting. It breathes slowly and regularly. Its stomach rises and falls with each breath. We need to become adept at breathing the way animals do when they are at rest. Spend a few minutes a day practicing. Stand in front of a full-length mirror. Place your hands lightly over your stomach. As you inhale, first allow your stomach to expand and then let your chest inflate. Do the reverse as you exhale slowly (fig. 6).

b. Another technique for your relaxation repertoire is *progressive relaxation*. Progressive relaxation is a method of learning to relax muscles through tension-relaxation contrast. What follows is a transcription of an audiotape by clinical psychologist Dr. John McCauley which I've found useful.

'Progressive relaxation is achieved by carefully and separately tensing each large muscle group, holding that tension for several seconds, and then relaxing the muscles you have tensed. If muscles are tense, they relax more deeply when they are released. The feeling of relaxation is increased by experiencing the contrast between extreme muscle tension and sudden release of that tension. To begin, get in a comfortable reclining position, preferably on a bed, and loosen any tight clothing. Legs and arms should be uncrossed when doing relaxation exercises. Legs are slightly apart and arms lie relaxed by your body. Fingers are slightly spread and not touching the rest of your body.

6   Place your hands lightly over your stomach. As you inhale, first allow your stomach to expand and then let your chest inflate. Do the reverse as you exhale slowly

'Start by opening your mouth and gently moving your jaw side to side. Close your mouth, keeping your teeth slightly apart. Take a deep breath into your stomach. As you exhale, feel yourself floating down into the bed like a limp rag doll.

'As you tighten one part of your body, try to leave the rest of your body limp and relaxed. When you tighten a body part, hold the tension for five seconds. Follow the release of tension by taking a deep breath. Hold that breath for five seconds, also, and then breathe out slowly.

'To get a clear understanding of the difference between tension and relaxation, begin by tensing every muscle in your body. Tense everything from your forehead to your feet. Then hold that tension. IN-CREASE that tension. Tense everywhere. When you finally let go, feel a wave of calm and a sense of relief as you release the tension.

'Start at your forehead. Wrinkle it up as tightly as you can. Feel the tension. Let the tension build for five seconds. Then let go. Follow by taking a deep breath, holding that for a few seconds, and then breathe out slowly.

'Continue this technique as you systematically work through your body. Start at your forehead, then move down to your eyes, jaws, neck, shoulders, arms, hands, chest, back, stomach, buttocks, legs, and feet. Remember to take a deep breath, hold it for five seconds and exhale slowly in between the tensing of each muscle group.

'Once you've worked your way through your body, mentally go back through these areas and allow them to feel more and more deeply relaxed. Search for any residual tension. If you find it, tense and relax that area again.'

c. Dr. McCauley describes a third relaxation technique for your program: *autogenic relaxation.* Autogenic training refers to the process by which an individual gives self-statements about relaxation. You passively allow the words to have an effect on you. To begin, get in a comfortable position similar to what you did for the progressive relaxation exercises.

Now take a deep slow breath. Hold your breath and tighten every body muscle until you feel your whole body start to tremble with tension. Then breathe out and let go completely. Repeat twice. Until you learn this material by heart, you might like to make a tape of the following phrases, spoken slowly in soothing tones, so that you can repeat them as you hear them. Concentrate on slow, deep breathing throughout.

I feel very calm and quiet.
I feel very comfortable and quiet.
I am beginning to feel quite relaxed.
I am beginning to feel quite relaxed.
My feet feel heavy and relaxed.
My feet feel heavy and relaxed.
My ankles feel heavy and relaxed.
My ankles feel heavy and relaxed.
My knees feel heavy and relaxed.
My knees feel heavy and relaxed.
My hips feel heavy and relaxed.
My hips feel heavy and relaxed.
My feet, my ankles, my knees, and my hips all feel heavy and relaxed.
My feet, my ankles, my knees, and my hips all feel heavy and relaxed.
My stomach and the whole center portion of my body feel heavy and relaxed.
My stomach and the whole center portion of my body feel heavy and relaxed.
My hands feel heavy and relaxed.
My hands feel heavy and relaxed.
My arms feel heavy and relaxed.
My arms feel heavy and relaxed.
My shoulders feel heavy and relaxed.
My shoulders feel heavy and relaxed.
My hands, my arms, and my shoulders all feel heavy and relaxed.
My hands, my arms, and my shoulders all feel heavy and relaxed.
My neck feels heavy and relaxed.
My neck feels heavy and relaxed.
My jaws feel heavy and relaxed.
My jaws feel heavy and relaxed.
My forehead feels heavy and relaxed.
My forehead feels heavy and relaxed.
My neck, my jaws, and my forehead all feel heavy and relaxed.
My neck, my jaws, and my forehead all feel heavy and relaxed.
My whole body feels heavy and relaxed.
My whole body feels heavy and relaxed.
My breathing is getting deeper and deeper.
My breathing is getting deeper and deeper.
I can feel the sun shining down on me warming the top of my head.
The top of my head feels warm and heavy.
The top of my head feels warm and heavy.

The relaxing warmth flows into my right shoulder.
My right shoulder feels warm and heavy.
My right shoulder feels warm and heavy.
My breathing is getting deeper and deeper.
The relaxing warmth flows down to my right hand.

My right hand feels warm and heavy.
My right hand feels warm and heavy.
The relaxing warmth flows back up to my right arm.
My right arm feels warm and heavy.
My right arm feels warm and heavy.
The relaxing warmth flows through my right elbow into my right shoulder.
My right elbow, my right shoulder feel warm and heavy.
My right elbow, my right shoulder feel warm and heavy.
(Repeat these last 13 lines for the left side of your body)

The relaxing warmth flows slowly throughout my whole back.
I feel the warmth relaxing my back.
My back feels warm and heavy.
My back feels warm and heavy.
My heart feels warm and easy.
My heart feels warm and easy.
My heart pumps relaxing warmth throughout my entire body.
My whole body is heavy, warm, and relaxed.
My whole body is heavy, warm, and relaxed.
I am breathing deeper and deeper.
My whole body feels very quiet and very serene.
My whole body feels very comfortable and very relaxed.
My mind is still.
My mind is quiet.
My mind is easy.
I withdraw my thoughts from my surroundings.
Nothing exists around me.
I feel serene, secure, still.
I am at ease, completely at ease.
Deep within my mind I can visualize and experience myself as relaxed.
I am comfortable and still.
My mind is calm and quiet.
I feel an inward peace.
I feel a new sense of well-being.[12]

Exercises to Enhance Visualization Skills

If you have difficulty imaging, the following exercises are suggested. They are listed starting with the simplest.

1. Close your eyes and count the windows in your house. In order to do this, you have to visualize all the walls and rooms of your house.

2. Drive to the local grocery store in your mind.

7   *Use your visualization skills and fill in all the details*

3. Imagine yourself flying (without a plane!).

4. Say the following words and take note of how you experience them. Try to actually see a picture in your mind's eye, hear a sound associated with the word — or smell, feel, or taste the word. Use all of your senses.

ocean	popcorn
snake	rain
summer	elevator
pizza	apple
rock music	friend

5. Additional exercises:

   a) Mentally examine the details of your favorite breeches.

   b) Mentally examine the details of your bridle.

   c) Visualize riding through your warm-up.

   d) Re-experience the most exciting thing that ever happened to you while riding.

   e) Visualize your tack room. Involve all of your senses.
   - How are the trunks arranged?
   - What is the color of the blankets?
   - What is the texture of the saddlepads?
   - Can you smell the leather?

6. Use visualization skills to improve riding skills (fig. 7). Examine all the details in your mind. See the shirt you are wearing and your horse's markings. Feel the contact on the reins. Is the footing hard or deep? What does the air smell like? Can you hear the rhythm of your horse's footfalls?
   Try the following mental exercises to enhance performance.

   a) Your horse is quick in the air over the jumps and as a result brings down rails behind. Visualize jumping clean in slow motion.

   b) You have a tendency to fling your upper body down over a fence. Picture the correct position on approach and see the horse jumping up to you to close the angle, rather than you ducking down.

   c) During your approach to a fence, your horse gets "behind" you. Imagine riding three-quarters of the horse out in front of you, using your legs as if squeezing toothpaste out of a tube (fig. 8).

8   *Imagine riding three-quarters of the horse out in front of you,*
    using your legs as if squeezing toothpaste out of a tube

d) Your horse swings his haunches out during shoulder-in.
   Visualize *only* the hind legs of the horse and see them
   traveling straight down the track.

e) Your transitions to the halt have been abrupt. Picture a
   snowflake drifting softly to the ground (fig. 9).

9 *Your transitions to the halt have been abrupt. Picture a
snowflake drifting softly to the ground*

Get Emotionally Involved

In addition to using your five senses when you picture your goals, make your images even more vivid by conjuring up strong, positive emotions. This works because intense feelings are the power behind an experience. (In a negative way, that is how phobias develop. Strong emotions become associated with an object or situation.)

So enhance your goals by being an active participant in your images rather than a passive observer. How can you do this? Think back. Can you remember a time when you were so excited that you could hardly sit still? Or how about the enthusiasm you felt on the day you got your first job or your new car? Or the exhilaration you felt when you won an important class?

If your memories don't evoke passionate feelings, take advantage of an emotion that you can experience vicariously. Picture the winning athletes at the Olympic Games as they watch their flag being raised and hear their national anthem being played. Feel their pride and the intensity of their emotions. All their years of dedication and effort culminate in this glorious moment. Imagine how they feel.

Or perhaps you'll have to wait until the next time you experience a positive emotion and then capture that feeling for the future. The situation does not have to be horse-related. All you need is a powerful emotion that you can use to your advantage. Then memorize the deep feeling and use it to strengthen the effect of your images.

Conclusion

To sum up, take advantage of this remarkable WIN mechanism that you possess. Realize that in struggles between the will and the imagination, imagination always prevails. If you, for instance, consider yourself to be a fat person, the will power used during a diet might work for the short term, but eventually your body will return to the size and shape you perceive yourself to be.

However, you don't have to rely on will power. Why struggle to overcome the power of imagination? Since our strong mental images largely determine our actions, go straight to the source to change your programming. Whatever you believe and vividly imagine will inevitably come to pass. Just think of the endless possibilities that will open up to you as you become adept at learning to WIN.

2

Win With Words

What You Say *Is* What You Get

As you acknowledge the power of words, realize that you can be "hung by your tongue." Once you verbalize either a positive or negative thought, you plant it in your mind. So be careful not to defeat yourself or impede your progress by the words you choose. Don't panic if negative thoughts pop into your mind (fig. 10). Regardless of your random thoughts, you don't give *power* to them unless you say the words out loud.

What you say is what you get. So be sure you want what you say. For instance, if you say, "I get bucked off every spring," then be prepared to get dumped. If you proclaim that "something always comes up to prevent me from getting to the first show of the season," it probably will. Or, "I'm broke. I never have the money to do what I want with my horse" — you won't. Instead make positive statements such as, "I'm very resourceful, and I *will* come up with the money I need," and you open your mind to discovering ways of raising that money. Perhaps your local club offers a scholarship. Or you can offer to pull manes in your barn for a fee. Or you can video other riders and be compensated for your time and equipment.

Ever think to yourself on the morning of a competition that you're exhausted because you've been up since 4 a.m. braiding? You feel that the best you can expect is that you won't ride well because you're so tired, and the worst-case scenario is that you'll probably forget your course or test because you're not thinking sharply.

Don't panic if these thoughts occur. Just ignore them, and above all don't verbalize them. Saying them aloud does the damage. Either say nothing or instead say, "I'm thrilled at how sharp I am, considering I've been up since 4 a.m. It must be all that wonderful adrenalin. I'm really excited to compete." You might not really feel this way, but it's better than verbalizing the opposite, which will seriously undermine your efforts.

10   Don't panic if negative thoughts pop into your mind

Experiment with the power of positive speech. On a dreary day say to whomever will listen (if only aloud to yourself) that you feel terrific! You feel energetic! You feel inspired to get a lot accomplished today. This proclamation can raise your spirits considerably. But even more importantly, you can avoid the converse—which is that by continuously complaining, you'll find it extremely difficult to get motivated.

When you ask my friend Jane Ashley how she is, she's never merely "fine." She always exclaims heartily, "I'm perfect!" And she is. She has the same aches, pains, and creaks that everyone else does. But she doesn't give her ailments power by dwelling on them and repeatedly verbalizing them.

The victim complains and feels overwhelmed. The winner knows he can't alter the facts, but he can always decide how he'll react to those facts and what he'll say. Victim or victor. It's your choice.

Jane Ashley suggests developing the cosmic perspective on losing. Look at the planets and recognize how insignificant we are and how unimportant this competition really is in the big picture

Censor Your Speech

I'm not saying that you can never express a negative. But if you must, do it in a way that helps rather than hurts you. For example, don't say you have a problem controlling your leg position. Instead, say, "I *used to* have a problem controlling my leg position, but I've been working on it and it's getting better."

Better yet, substitute the word "challenge" for the word "problem." Saying you have a challenge controlling your leg position conjures an image of working through something you are sure you can overcome. "Problem," on the other hand, conjures an image of being defeated by something beyond your control. You know from our discussion of psychocybernetics the importance of the images you plant in your mind. If you want to harvest carrots, don't plant weeds! Sow positive, goal-oriented seeds if you want to harvest success.[1]

Since words are such powerful allies or enemies, it is best to choose your 'friends' wisely. Be your own censor. Listen carefully to what you say. Are you a complainer? Do you always look at the dark side? Do you hear your self-sabotage? "I can't believe I was so stupid to forget to go through the finish flags at the end of the course. I always make at least one dumb mistake like that in every stadium round." "Every time I start a leg-yield I stiffen through my whole body, and then my horse can't even trot freely." "I'm going to make a fool of myself if I go to that show because all the professionals will be in my division, and I'll be totally outclassed." Think before you speak and avoid the damaging words.

Build your awareness of the kind of words you use. Take two or three days and keep track of how many negatives you express. Include even things like complaints about the weather or your health. Jot down the number of times these words tumble out. You might be surprised at how negative you really are. Don't get depressed by this realization. Before you can do something about a problem, you have to recognize its existence. So get excited about this increase in your self-awareness. It's the first step towards using the power of words to your advantage.

A by-product of building your awareness of words is that you also begin to really hear what others say. That's important. You want to limit your exposure to the influences of negative people. But before you can avoid these influences, you have to be able to identify them.

Do some verbal house-cleaning in which you sweep certain words out of your vocabulary (fig. 11). Sweep out words like depressed, discouraged, and frustrated. They can only hurt you. Eliminating such words will not only improve your riding substantially, but will also improve the quality of your life. Rather than being *depressed* that you haven't been able to ride consistently, get *excited* about the prospect of an upcoming clinic. Rather than being *discouraged* by slow progress, get *exhilarated* by what you have learned and the prospect of improving through a lifetime of learning. Rather than being *frustrated* that your horse is not going well, *look forward enthusiastically* to getting the help that is going to turn it around for you.

11 *Do some verbal housecleaning in which you sweep certain words out of your vocabulary*

Cindy Sydnor believes that when the joy and grace are missing in riding and training, we've missed the point

Also, eliminate the word "try" from your vocabulary. When you "try" to do something, it sounds like a half-hearted effort. Don't try to do your best. *Do* your best. Don't try to ride a good haunches-in. *Ride* a good haunches-in.

"If" is another powerful little word that does a lot of damage. It denotes a lack of conviction and belief in yourself. When you hear an "if" trying to escape, substitute a "when." *If* I could just control my hands . . . becomes *when* I learn to control my hands.

If I could just make it around stadium clean . . . becomes *when* I make it around stadium clean. *If* I could find the time to practice . . . becomes *when* I find the time to practice.

You can also censor the "if's" that others direct towards you. When someone says, "Now, Suzie, 'if' you do well at this show, you'll be qualified for the Regional Finals," stop them cold. Your response should be, "What do you mean, 'if'? *When* I do well at this show, I'll be qualified for the Regionals."

"Can't" is another good word to dump. Just because you haven't done something before doesn't mean you can't. Remember, if you think you can or you can't, you're right. Such a little word can do so much harm. "Can't" shows a lack of belief in yourself. *Believing something can be done and believing you can do it is basic to the successful application of WIN techniques.*

When using words to help you achieve your goals, express yourself with positive statements. Rather than saying, "I won't be nervous," say, "I will be relaxed." Claim it, and its yours. Successful riders don't wait for things to happen. They make things happen by deciding what they want and declaring it in a positive way. "I will master this exercise." "I will compete successfully at the Radnor Three Day Event this fall."

Instead of saying:	Substitute:
I'm going to *try* to do my best at the show today.	I'm going to do my best at the show today.
I haven't competed at First Level because my horse *can't* lengthen his stride at the trot.	I'm working on developing my horse's trot lengthenings so we can soon compete at First Level.
I do fine at the event during dressage and cross-country, but every time I ride into stadium, *I freeze and make all kinds of mistakes.*	I used to freeze in the stadium phase of my event, but I've been working with my instructor and I'm getting so much better.
I have a *problem* because I sit crookedly on my horse.	It's a *challenge* for me to sit straight, but I'm definitely improving.
If I stay relaxed during my round, I can help my horse jump clean.	*When* I stay relaxed during my round, I can help my horse jump clean.
I *won't* stiffen during half-pass.	I will stay loose through my body during half-pass.
I'm a *timid* rider.	I used to be a timid rider, but I'm getting braver as I become more experienced.
I'm so *discouraged* about the way my horse is going.	I'm excited about having my lesson this week so I can improve the way my horse is going.

Positive Self-Talk

It's a bonus to have a good support group. But even if you do, be your own cheerleader, too. Engage in positive self-talk. "The greatest conversation you have every day is with yourself . . . so do it with all due respect."[2] When doubts creep in, give yourself a pep talk. "Hey, I know this is tough competition, but I'm really ready. I've done my homework, my horse and I have a special partnership, and I'm excited to show these judges just what we're capable of."

Words spoken at random effect us. Therefore, control your language. *Never* put yourself down. Your self-image is always listening to what you say about about yourself. Maltz says, "Don't downgrade the product simply because you haven't used it correctly. That's like the schoolboy who complains his typewriter can't spell."

Do you feel odd talking yourself up? So what? If it works and makes you feel better, do it.

Do you feel arrogant saying things like that? You shouldn't. Understand that not only do you have a responsibility to yourself to be the best you can be, but also you aren't boasting about something others can't do, too. They are just as free to put the same success principles into practice.

Robert Dover is one of the United States' most successful dressage riders. He is familiar to dressage enthusiasts everywhere for his participation in the World Championships on Federleicht (1986) and Waltzertakt (1990), the Olympics on Romantico (1984) and Juvel and Federleicht (1988), and the World Cup on Federleicht (1986 and 1987). While competing in Europe Robert became the first American in 30 years to win International Grand Prix and Kurs, and in 1987 he was the leader of the European League for the World Cup.

Robert uses the power of positive speaking very cleverly throughout his training and competing. He has dealt with a variety of horses with diverse physical difficulties and mental quirks. But regardless of which horse he is on at the moment, he proclaims enthusiastically and with tremendous conviction that "this horse is a genius." Or, "this horse is not only the most talented horse in the country . . . but probably in the world."

Robert good-naturedly takes the teasing that goes along with those kinds of statements. "Hey, Robert! Not only is this the best horse in the country if not the world . . . but probably the galaxy if not the universe!" Robert is totally aware of what he is doing by his choice of words. He is programming himself for success. You, too, can use the power of positive speaking in the same way as this Olympian does.

Regardless of which horse he is on at the moment, Robert Dover proclaims enthusiastically that "this horse is a genius"

Capture the Power of Words

Depending on my immediate goal, I like to experiment with various powerful words. It's fun to shape my attitude or my day with particular words. One day I might drive to the barn repeating over and over the word "harmony" (fig. 12). As a result balance and lightness predominate. "Self-carriage" is another favorite that I use to set the tone of the day's session.

To this day I am still intrigued by the tremendous power of words. As an example, years ago I was showing a horse at Third Level. He was a talented horse but quite lazy. It was a hot day, and as soon as I started the test, I felt him not wanting to go forward. I knew the test wasn't going to be brilliant. I quickly thought about what I could do to salvage the ride. So, I thought, "We might not be brilliant, but we can be *accurate and polished*." Throughout the ride, I kept repeating those two words. Imagine my amazement when I walked out of the arena, and the first person I spoke to was a spectator who used those *exact* words to describe my ride! Evidently I was able to convey the essence of those words in my performance by simply repeating them to myself.

Cindy Sydnor, Grand Prix dressage rider and trainer from Brae-burn Farm in Snow Camp, North Carolina, is best known for her classically correct position on a horse. Her riding is the epitome of beauty and elegance, and her philosophy is expressed by her desire "to set an example to a few who might watch and think, 'What a nice picture she and her horse make! They both look happy and graceful.' When the joy and grace are missing, we've missed the point."

Inspired by her example, I decided to try to capture the feeling of Cindy's riding at another competition by using her name as a catch-word. So, I rode into a qualifying class repeating her name—Cindy, Cindy, Cindy—while picturing her clearly in my mind's eye. To my amazement, as I left the arena, one of the spectators (who is also a dressage judge) said to me, "I hope you win that class. That was a lovely ride. You reminded me so much of Cindy Sydnor!"

Another way to capture the power of words is to pick a word or phrase that appeals to you. How about "joyful," "effortless," "rhythm," "brave," "aggressive," or "smooth as silk"? Write the word or phrase down on a couple of 3″ x 5″ cards. Put these cards in places where you'll see them often. I personally find the refrigerator a good spot. Your bathroom mirror or the sun visor in your car are also likely places. Look at your word whenever you can. Repeat it aloud as frequently as possible. And get ready for some exciting changes in your riding.

12   *One day I might drive to the barn repeating the word "harmony" over and over*

3

WIN with the As If *Principle*

The *As If* Principle is a wonderful tool to use during the process of becoming the very best rider, trainer, and competitor you can be. Simply stated, if you want to possess a quality, act "as if" you already do, and it will soon become yours.[1]

If you want to be a poised competitor, act "as if" you are gracious and relaxed. If you want to be a confident trainer, act "as if" you are self-assured. If you want to be free from fear, act "as if" you are courageous. Whatever trait you desire, act "as if" you already possess it, and eventually you will. "You do not sing because you are happy, you are happy because you sing. *Physical expressions feed mental acceptance.*"[2]

On the other hand, if you act "as if" you're nervous at competitions, or if you act "as if" you're insecure about your abilities to school your horse, or if you panic every time your horse is disobedient, then your tension, insecurity, and fear become a reality as well. "Each of us becomes that make-believe self that we have imagined and fantasized most."[3] Do you see yourself "as if" you're a champion? A patient and tolerant trainer? A rider who demonstrates love and respect for the horse?

Psychocybernetics and the *As If* Principle

Add the *As If* Principle to your practice of psychocybernetics. Set a goal, visualize your objective *"as if" it were already in existence*, and act "as if" it were impossible to fail. If your goal is to finish among the top five riders in the One Hundred Mile Endurance Ride, go through the necessary preparations and conditioning "as if" your victory were a foregone conclusion. Each day set aside some time to visualize your horse finishing in peak condition. Or if your goal is to compete successfully at your first Three Day Event, fill out your entry form, diligently prepare your horse, learn all the rules and how to do your timing on speed and endurance, and organize your clothing and equipment "as if" there were not a doubt in your mind that you will be totally ready when the time comes. And then vividly and repeatedly imagine completing the event without jumping faults and with a sound horse.

Dr. Denis Waitley, President of the La Jolla Clinic Research Foundation, is the author of *The Psychology of Winning, The Winner's Edge*, and *The Double Win*. Dr. Waitley holds a Ph.D. in human behavior and has done extensive work with Olympic athletes.

In his work, Dr. Waitley supports the use of the *As If* Principle combined with psychocybernetics. He firmly believes that by establishing a clearly-defined goal—dwelling on it morning and night with words, pictures, and emotions "as if" you had already achieved it—your WIN mechanism will move you purposefully in that direction.

Using the *As If* Principle to Handle Show-Nerves

Years ago I decided to put the *As If* Principle to the test and determine for myself if acting in a certain way at competitions would eventually change my thinking and the way I truly felt. When I

Act 'as if' you're Virginia Leng, so you can remove your own limitations and ride as she would

started to compete, I was very nervous. I remember not sleeping well the night before a show. I vividly recall the stomach and intestinal disorders I experienced the day of the show. Resolving to do something about this unpleasant condition, I acted "as if" I was not nervous. I acted "as if" I was calm, confident, and poised. Temporarily I was still anxious, but my demeanor was self-assured. Friends would ask if I ever got nervous. I would confidently proclaim, "No, I rarely get nervous. I love to compete. In fact, I'm concerned if I'm not charged up a little because I rely on my adrenalin to give me an edge."

Then one day it occurred to me that I hadn't been nervous for quite awhile. I was sleeping well before competitions, and, much to my relief, my intestinal troubles had ceased. I was actually enjoying the entire competitive experience.

Apparently, by assuming the characteristics of a seasoned, calm competitor, I had become one. Since the mind/body connection can not be separated, I had been able to change the way I felt simply by changing the way I acted.

Assuming Desirable Qualities

Earl Nightengale, motivational speaker and author of *This is Earl Nightengale*, says, "We, literally, become what we think about most of the time. As you see yourself in your mind's eye ... so you do become."[4] What kind of rider, trainer, or competitor do you see yourself as? Do you like what you see? If you're not satisfied, make some changes: Would you like to be a patient trainer, a confident rider, or a poised competitor? Start acting today "as if" you are, and you'll be on your way to making some exciting discoveries.

Enthusiasm

How would you like to enhance every moment of your time spent with your horse? It's simple. Become an enthusiastic person. Enthusiasm is a wonderful quality and a powerful tool. You say by nature you are kind of quiet and low key? Well, develop enthusiasm by acting "as if" you are enthusiastic. You don't know how? Study enthusiastic people. Listen to what they say and how they say it. Watch how they walk with vitality. Notice that smiling and laughing are the rule for them rather than the exception.

When someone asks you if you are looking forward to the next competition, don't say that you are worried, not prepared, and sure to embarrass yourself. Instead, enthusiastically proclaim that you are psyched! You can't wait! It's going to be a blast!

If your horse hasn't been going well in your daily schooling, don't get frustrated. See your dilemma as a wonderful opportunity for growth. Your difficulties will motivate you to seek answers rather than just carry on at a comfortable but mediocre standard. For example, perhaps you'll borrow a video camera so you can tape your ride and get some feedback. Study the tape to see if you can pinpoint the problem yourself or share it with a professional who can give you some insight.

Enthusiastic expectations become self-fulfilling prophecy. If you expect to get nothing from a lesson or show, you'll get just that. If you expect to have fun, you will. What you get out of your time and experiences with your horse will be in direct proportion to your enthusiasm. As Dr. Waitley says in his *Psychology of Winning*, "You may or may not get what is coming to you or what you deserve . . . but you will nearly always get what you expect."

You can prove to yourself that the *As If* Principle exists. Pick a day when you feel a little blue. Then, act "as if" you're happy. Walk with a bounce in your stride. Talk enthusiastically. Force yourself to smile. Better yet, dig deep and bring forth a huge belly laugh. Don't be surprised when you feel your spirits lift.

Courage

It is reasonable to think that we might occasionally be afraid of getting hurt while dealing with our horses. We are working with creatures that outweigh us often by eight to ten times, and their actions are not governed by logic. Feeling threatened or out of control can be a very stressful state.

If you are going to enjoy your horse, it's important not to be overwhelmed and paralyzed by your fears. Horses are sensitive animals, and if you are afraid, they will sense your anxiety. Transmitting your fear will only increase your horse's tension.

So, in order to become a bold, fearless person, act "as if" you are aggressive and confident. Action cures fear. When successful riders encounter fear, they admit it and go on in spite of it. If you do the very thing you fear, you destroy that fear. On the other hand, if you give in to your fears, dwell on them, and visualize the worst, eventually you will create the very conditions that frighten you. An old proverb says, "That which you fear and expect the most will surely come to pass. The body manifests what the mind harbors."[5]

Let's say you are intimidated by drop jumps. Each time you worry about going over a drop, the fence looms larger and larger. Soon, in your imagination, you are jumping into the Grand Canyon (fig. 13). You try self-persuasion. You tell yourself drops are physically no more difficult than any other jump and all horses manage to get their landing gear down. So what if you fall off? When you really think about it, it's only a few feet to the ground. All your arguments, however, fail to quiet your queasy stomach. In fact, the more you dwell on the prospect of this jump, the more anxious you get.

13 *You worry about going over a drop fence. Soon, in your imagination, you are jumping into the Grand Canyon*

Well, stop thinking about it and just go and do it. Attack that fence "as if" you are an international Three Day Event Champion like Bruce Davidson. Ride confidently and aggressively. You'll find that the mental monster you have created with your fear shrinks to manageable proportions.

I'm not suggesting that you act in a foolhardy way. You should take all reasonable precautions. Wear a safety helmet. Don't overface yourself or your horse. Do only what your education and experience to that point have prepared you for. Be under professional supervision. Then, when you are properly prepared, go for it "as if" your whole heart is in it.

Maria L. understands the magic of acting "as if" you are fearless. One day while schooling over cross-country fences, she and her horse had quite a dramatic fall. They came too fast and too flat into a ditch with a large fence over it. Maria's horse stepped into the ditch, chested the fence, and flipped. Maria was first catapulted over the fence, and when her horse flipped he landed on her. The fall was particularly scary, but Maria knew she had to act "as if" she were not frightened. Making sure all parts of both horse and rider were undamaged, she quickly remounted. Taking advantage of the fact that action cures fear, she immediately followed a systematic plan of action. She did this under the watchful eye of her trainer.

They started with a Novice-level ditch that was narrow at one end and got progressively wider. Maria jumped back and forth without stopping. Over and over she jumped while her trainer perfected her technique. As her technique improved, she gradually jumped the wider parts of the little ditch.

Next, they progressed to a larger ditch, but one without a fence over it. Maintaining her momentum, Maria jumped back and forth until her technique was solid. When her trainer thought the moment was right, she had Maria continue over the original big ditch with the fence.

Maria acted "as if" she were bold and aggressive, and she became bold and aggressive. So much so, that just weeks later she successfully and easily competed in her first Preliminary Horse Trials.

Patience

As a patient trainer, you act and react to your horse with tolerance and understanding. Your motto is "I have time." You are satisfied and encouraged with little bits of measurable progress because you know that all those little bits add up over time to a great deal of progress. You don't lose your temper because you realize that "violence begins where knowledge ends." Therefore, *you* take the responsibility for a bad ride rather than blaming your horse. If you had more knowledge or were more experienced, you'd be able to help your horse through his difficulties. The deficiency is in you, not in the horse, so it's unfair to take your frustrations out on him.

Over time, as you act "as if" you're a patient trainer, you'll discover that you become one. Your horse does not become an innocent victim of your ego and lack of self-control. Your rides become more harmonious and satisfying for both you and your horse. You both leave each session with a sense of accomplishment.

Poise

The poised competitor acts "as if" everything is progressing smoothly and according to plan. You are aware of show management hassles, such as running behind schedule or inadequate footing, but you are minimally disturbed by these things.

Other competitors do not adversely affect you. You can be whole-heartedly happy about their successes because what they do has little to do with your personal progress with your horse. Competition boils down to *showing* where you're at in your training. Show where you are with pride and joy. By acting "as if" you are poised, you'll become that way, and you'll add immensely to the fun of competing.

Confidence

While remaining open-minded and receptive to constructive criticism, a successful rider maintains a confident demeanor throughout the work. Learn to ignore that little voice inside you that second-guesses and downgrades your abilities.

If you doubt yourself, your horse is not going to take you seriously. Horses are notoriously clever at testing insecure riders (and behaving beautifully when ridden by a professional). Acknowledge that every second you are riding you are either training or untraining your horse. If your lack of confidence causes you to be passive or to hesitate before making corrections, you are teaching your horse to be disobedient. So if he moves around while you're trying to mount, get off. Insist that he stands completely still while you get on and that he waits for the signal from you before he walks off. Or, if he adopts a rhythm that is hurried and chaotic, don't wait to take action. Steady him immediately and then insist he goes at the pace you determine.

Be decisive and firm. Perhaps you'll occasionally make the wrong decision, but you will know that from the feedback you get from your horse. So, by acting "as if" you are confident, you will instill a quiet authority into your work and your horse will respect you.

Discipline

Rarely is there success without discipline. We're so attuned to instant gratification that sometimes it is difficult to adhere to the demands of a long-term program. So, even if you are completely disorganized, start acting "as if" you are disciplined. Organize yourself and commit yourself to your priorities. Become more orderly throughout your day, your exercise, your eating habits, your work, and your schooling sessions. Soon it will become second nature — and anything else will feel like chaos.

So, *you choose*. Pick a quality you desire. Bold, dedicated, or elegant. Act "as if" you already possess that quality, and get ready for some exciting changes.

Confidence and concentration are part of the winning formula for international Three Day Event Champion, Bruce Davidson

4

Positively Riding

Attitude

Ever heard yourself saying, "I know I can't keep my horse balanced in extensions"? Or, "I know we can't make it around that course clean"? Or, "I know I'll never qualify for the finals with this horse"? And, of course, you're unsuccessful because your outcomes were determined before you even began. Success or failure started with your thinking rather than your doing. Your attitude is so powerful that it dictates the following: if you think you can or you can't, you're right.

Consider that throughout the entire history of sports up to the year 1954, athletes were unable to run a mile in under four minutes. This feat was perceived as a physical impossibility. Then along came Roger Bannister who believed he could break this barrier — and he did. The interesting fact is that once Bannister succeeded, athletes all over the world were able to do the same. Man had not physically changed that much. The barrier was broken because it was a mental obstacle rather than a physical one. Once runners believed it could be done, they did it time and time again. Their attitude made all the difference.[1]

When I first started riding with a dressage coach and trainer in 1980, I was sorely tempted to ask him if he thought I had what it took to be a good rider and trainer. I admired him tremendously, so his opinion was important to me. The question almost got asked many times. What stopped me from asking was that it occurred to me that as much as I admired my trainer, it didn't matter what he thought. What mattered was my attitude — what *I* thought. Did *I* think I was capable of becoming a good rider? My own thinking would determine my limitations. As soon as I realized this fact, my need to ask the question (and hopefully receive his affirmation) was gone.

With the right attitude you can overcome obstacles that seem insurmountable. Take, for example, the story of John, a student of mine who worked as a stable hand.

John was extremely insecure. His self-esteem was so low that it had taken him a year just to build up the nerve to ask me for a lesson. He had a severe learning disability and as a result both his teachers and his peers had categorized and labeled him as mildly retarded. The teacher of the "Special Ed" course he took to improve his basic communication skills pronounced that he would never read or write beyond the sixth-grade level, so there was no point even bothering with further education.

In addition, he had to overcome the handicap of having little emotional support for his horse endeavors. A typical comment from his family was, "When are you going to quit playing with these horses, settle down, and get a real job?"

To make things worse, John's horse was physically stiff and needed a lot of reschooling. Plus, the horse had such a negative attitude towards work that if John used his legs, his horse would pin his ears back and kick out.

All of these factors stacked the odds overwhelmingly against John's achieving any level of success in his riding. But what he did have in his favor was a terrific attitude. He was eager, enthusiastic, and hungry to learn. And, he was willing to work hard and do whatever was necessary to improve.

Tacie Saltonstall finds that giving herself the gift of time to ride is what enables her to give so much to everyone else around her

Amazingly, after two years, John brought his horse from a very poor Second Level to a solid Prix St. Georges. He competed successfully and even held his own with the professionals at big, recognized shows. This was quite an accomplishment for anyone — let alone someone with so many obstacles to overcome.

The point is that with his attitude of determination and positive expectation, John's limitations were incidental. I'll take someone with a handicap and the right attitude any day over the person with all the advantages and a poor attitude.

Self-Image

John's success with his horse contributed substantially to a change in his self-image. Once he saw himself as worthy and competent, he was able to pursue confidently other goals such as his new job.

This is an important point because, although a positive attitude contributes to success, positive thinking *cannot* work unless you have a good self-image. If you are unhappy with your performance, you must improve your self-image. You can not perform consistently when it is inconsistent with the way you see yourself.

Maltz says, "All your actions, feelings, and behavior — even your abilities — are always consistent with your self-image. You will 'act like' the sort of person you conceive yourself to be . . . You literally can not act otherwise, in spite of all your conscious efforts or will power . . . The self-image prescribes the limits for the accomplishment of goals. It prescribes the 'area of the possible'."

Fortunately, you have a way to change your self-image through the use of psychocybernetic principles. Since your WIN mechanism seeks to achieve the pictures created in your imagination, make the development of a healthy self-image your primary goal. See yourself as competent and deserving. Imagine yourself confident and able to succeed at whatever project you undertake. Since the subconscious hears and believes everything you say, use the power of positive speech to improve your self-image. Once you develop a sound self-image, your subsequent goals will be more readily attainable.

Cancel the Negative

We live in a negative world. All you have to do is listen to the news, pick up a newspaper, or listen to your friends and co-workers to be deluged with negativity. Nothing will destroy your attitude more quickly than listening to and verbalizing negatives. Knowing how important your attitude is to success, take steps to zealously preserve positive thinking.

You need a plan to deal with all this negativity. Einstein says it takes "eleven or more correct inputs to negate erroneous information (fig. 14). In other words, it takes many right thinking deposits to overcome 'stinkin thinkin' deposits."[2] So make a concerted effort to cancel the negative. Maintain a positive balance by getting deliberate input from good books, motivational tapes, and uplifting movies. Listen to and be around positive people. Be aware of the company you keep. Negative thinking is like a disease. It is very contagious. Refuse to be infected. Walk away from people who would bring you down to their level. Instead, seek out those with positive, enthusiastic outlooks on life.

14   *It takes eleven or more correct inputs to negate erroneous information*

15 Visualize a transparent shield around yourself. Then picture the negative words of others hitting the shield and being deflected

I use a few tricks to protect myself from being bombarded by negative thoughts. If the thoughts and words come from people around me, I visualize a transparent shield around myself. It looks like a glass bubble. Then I picture the actual words hitting the invisible shield and being deflected (fig. 15). I know I cannot stop others from spewing their negatives—but I can protect myself and my attitude from harm. I remain safely within the vacuum of my glass bubble.

Thought-Stopping

If the negative comes from within, I employ a technique called "thought-stopping." It can enable you to foil your negative thoughts in a variety of ways. For instance, when you find yourself thinking negative, defeatist thoughts, visualize drawing a big black X right through the words or mental image. That will put an end to the destructive influence.

So the next time you "see" your horse shying at the trailer at the end of the dressage arena or refusing to jump the ditch on the cross-country course, draw a huge X through your negative mental picture. Refuse to give power to the image.

Another method is to visualize a blackboard. On it are the negative thoughts and images going through your mind. See yourself take an eraser and wipe the board clean. Then look at the clean slate and fill it with positive, helpful words or images (fig. 16).

16　*See yourself taking an eraser and wiping the board clean.
Then look at the clean slate and fill it with positive,
helpful words or images*

Or study a roadside stop sign for a good solid minute. Memorize its shape, color, and letters. Get an indelible picture of this stop sign in your mind's eye. Then whenever negative thoughts or pictures enter your mind, block them out by holding up the stop sign in your imagination.

If you want to get more actively involved in ridding your mind of all the garbage that pops into it, try writing down all your negatives, doubts, and insecurities on a piece of paper. Then take this paper and throw it in the trash! That's where all that garbage belongs anyhow. Your actions are symbolic of your change in thinking.

Worry

To preserve your attitude, you need to banish worry from your life. "Worry is a misuse of imagination."[3] Worry is a nonproductive emotion. Worrying would make sense if it were capable of changing the situation. All worry can do is depress you and clog your creativity. Worry creates failure. If you habitually worry about your horse refusing certain jumps, or worry about him shying when out on the trail, or worry that he'll be overexcited and disobedient at the show — then you're setting yourself up to fail. As you worry, you often imagine these dire things. Since your subconscious mind can't tell the difference between real and imagined failure, your worrying can backfire because your nondiscriminating WIN mechanism will actually help you accomplish what you've agonized about.

If you *must* worry, schedule your worry time. Allow yourself the luxury of worrying once a day for a twenty-minute period. And then worry your head off! . . . Worry that your horse might come up lame. Worry that the blacksmith won't show up before your horse's shoes fall off. Worry that your horse will pick up the wrong lead at the show this weekend. Pour your heart and soul into worrying about everything troubling you. Then, when your twenty minutes are over, time's up (fig. 17).

Perhaps the start of your designated worry time is noon. If you start worrying about something in the morning, put it out of your mind until noon. At noon, worry as hard as you can for your allotted twenty minutes. If you begin to worry again that afternoon or evening, tell yourself you'll just have to wait until noon the following day before you can think about it.

17   Allow yourself the luxury of worrying once a day for a
     twenty-minute period. And worry your head off! . . .

. . . Then, when your twenty minutes are over, time's up!

Sources of Inspiration

Take out an inner insurance policy for the preservation of your positive attitude. Do this by searching for sources of inspiration. Find a favorite quotation or catch phrase that you can say to yourself when things get rough. One of my favorites is: "You would not be given the dream without the means whereby." It always makes me feel that whatever I dream is within the realm of possibility. The way may not always be obvious, but it exists, and your WIN mechanism will help provide the "means whereby." Believe you are resourceful and know that inside you there are very many untapped abilities and undeveloped talents.

Another favorite quote that inspires me is: "Whatever the mind of man can conceive and believe, it can achieve."[4] No goal is out of reach if you believe you can attain it. The fact that we can fly, talk on the telephone, and see pictures through a box called television is the result of people having a vision, believing in it, and achieving it through work. So, if you've thought about eventing at the preliminary level, and you believe that you and your horse are capable, take the necessary steps to prepare and go do it.

When things get tough, try thinking, "Keep on keeping on." When your horse repeatedly breaks down, when your instructor has just moved to another state, and when vet bills are draining your lesson funds — keep on keeping on. Persistence pays off, and eventually you'll come out on top.

Inspiration can come in many forms. Yours might be a photo that you hang in a place where you'll see it often. Or perhaps a phone call or visit to someone who always helps you see things from the 'possibility point of view.' I have a ten-minute segment from an inspiring movie that I play over and over when I want to get myself psyched. How about "inspiration by association"?[5] In other words, as we discussed earlier, keep company with dynamic, positive people rather than negative complainers.

Criticism

Criticism can be positive or negative. The value of the former goes without saying. However, even negative feedback can be helpful *if* it guides you to correct your course. For instance, your instructor might tell you that to ride more effectively, you must spend time on the longe line improving your seat. Or that you need more mileage at your current competitive level before advancing to the next stage.

When facing criticism that is not constructive, don't allow your attitude to take a beating by being overly sensitive to the remarks of others. Be selective about whose criticism you take seriously. If the person is someone whose opinion you respect, use the critical comments in a positive way that permits you to grow.

How seriously, however, should you consider the opinion of the armchair trainer who has never schooled a horse, when he tells you that you don't have the ability to progress beyond Second Level? Or do you really think a friend who stables a horse in the same barn as you and just hacks for pleasure knows when you are ready to move up to the Intermediate level of eventing? So you must consider the source carefully when you listen to critical input, and use your own judgment in weighing the advice.

There will be times to ignore even the remarks of knowledgeable people — so-called experts in the field. The dressage world should be grateful that Cindy Sydnor chose to ignore the discouraging words of a well-respected judge. At Cindy's first competition she was advised to "quit riding and take up knitting." Fortunately, Cindy knew what she wanted and refused to be disheartened. If she had listened to the criticism she received, it would have been a loss to all who are now influenced by the grace and poise she displays as rider, trainer, competitor, and judge.

Often nonconstructive criticism from others stems from their own personal problems. Because negative people usually aren't excited and happy themselves, their frame of reference is distorted. They try to feel powerful by bringing you down to their level. "There is no way you will ever make that horse better." "There is no way you'll ever qualify for the championships." Perhaps that is true for *them* but only because they think on that level. Don't let someone else decide what you can or cannot do — or how much fun you will or will not have with your horse.

Remember, you are the only one who can give someone permission to make you feel bad or inadequate about your riding. Refuse to give someone that power over you. Take responsibility. It's not true that *he made me* feel badly when he said that ... It's that *I let myself* feel badly when he said that.

Loser's Limp

Excuses might be a wonderful way to save face, but they don't do your attitude a whole lot of good. Your excuse is your handy *loser's limp*.[6] "I started riding when I was too old." "My left leg is an inch shorter than my right leg." "I could not ride for four days before that show." In your effort to save face, you give yourself permission to fail. If you're going to defeat yourself before you even mount up, you might as well leave your horse in the barn. Understand that every time you use an excuse, it gains power. It becomes more deeply embedded in your subconscious mind. "Thoughts, positive or negative, grow stronger when fertilized with constant repetition."[7] What's your loser's limp? Are you too old, young, fat, poor, busy, sick, tired, or stressed out to have fun and ride well?

Inner Strength

Nancy Bliss valiantly displays courage by refusing to use a physical disability as a loser's limp. Nancy is a top Three Day Event rider from New England. In 1980 she was the Junior National Champion as well as the United States Combined Training Association Leading Young Rider. In 1982 she and her horse Cobblestone proudly represented the United States as a member of the Three Day team that captured the bronze medal at the World Championships in Luhmulen, Germany. Nancy had a promising future as she prepared for the 1984 Olympics with the now veteran Cobblestone and her second mount, Rio Doge. Unfortunately, at the National Open Championships at Chesterland in Unionville, Pennsylvania, in 1983, she started to experience some bizarre physical symptoms.

Nancy describes what happened at Chesterland as follows: "Dressage went really well for both horses. Cobble was in the top five and I believe Doge was thirteenth. Cobble was great cross-country, but this was Doge's first Advanced Three Day Event, and I knew I needed to be able to help him. As I trotted out on Roads and Tracks, part of the Endurance Phase, I felt a strange sensation in my legs. I kept squeezing my thighs — testing to see if I could finish the ride. As it turned out Doge went fabulously, but I was really tired.

"I remember lying in bed that night and my legs were numb. It wasn't painful — just scary. The next day I tried to sleep a lot in the tack room. I still felt extremely weak in my legs. In fact, when it came time to ride I couldn't get on my horse. My groom, Polly, had to help me mount. But Doge did well, as we had only one rail down. I was

Nancy Bliss did not just quietly fade away when she was diagnosed with multiple sclerosis — she went on to coach young champions and returned to three day eventing herself

really happy to have placed tenth with him in his first Advanced Three Day and third with Cobble.

"During the drive home I kept banging on my legs. I said, 'Watch this, Polly, I can't feel this' — like it was a big joke.

"My legs got progressively worse. I remember driving to a clinic that I was going to teach and feeling as if my feet were blowing up and that they were going to blow my shoes off. Then I started to have trouble with my left hand. I had no strength. My fingers kept opening and I'd drop the rein.

"While all of this was going on and I was waiting to get an appointment with a medical specialist, the U. S. Equestrian Team came out with their Long-List for the 1984 Olympics and I was named to it!"

Nancy was diagnosed in November of 1983 with multiple sclerosis. Doctors unfamiliar with the demands of her sport said she could continue to ride, but she should avoid physical and emotional stress. For an Olympic hopeful, avoiding stress is not compatible with the rigors of eventing. Above all, she had to prevent any chance of injury to her spinal cord. However, she continued to compete and in 1984 at the Kentucky Three Day Event the worst happened — she had a disastrous fall and fractured her neck.

Faced with these misfortunes, Nancy's positive attitude is truly inspirational. She is unfailingly cheerful and optimistic. Naturally her disappointment at being unable to make the Olympic team in 1984 was considerable. She said, "Once you step up on a podium and receive a medal, you never want to step down." But she never had a moment of self-pity. In fact, she found it easier to come to terms with her own disease than to deal with other people who were feeling sorry for her. She had to work hard at letting them know she was okay.

This plucky athlete never uses multiple sclerosis as an excuse to settle for less than her best. I remember giving her a lesson during which I frequently had to correct the position of her left hand. I had forgotten she had no feeling in this hand, and at times it would just open and the rein would fall through. Rather than make excuses, she told me to keep reminding her about it. She claimed that if she thought about it, she could correct it with her mind rather than her muscle.

Nancy knows she will always have multiple sclerosis, but she doesn't let this slow her down. She is currently in remission and experiences no obvious debilitating symptoms. She follows a maintenance program of eating a proper diet, staying fit by biking, riding, and running up to four miles per day, and trying not to stress herself by getting overtired.

Her impact on the sport of eventing continues. At Hermit Hill Farm in Lyme, New Hampshire she coaches serious Three Day Event students. She has produced North American Young Rider champions, Wendy and Nini Stevenson. She has competed several horses through Training Level, and in 1987 she rode in her first Three Day Event since her accident. Nancy Bliss did not just quietly fade away.

Strength of Will

Physical challenges can take other forms. I remember watching a woman with one arm compete in a dressage show. She had one rein attached to an apparatus on the empty sleeve of her right arm. When it came time to do the free walk on a long rein, she deftly moved the rein to another hook further down her sleeve so that her horse could stretch his neck. At the end of the diagonal, she smoothly reattached the rein to the shorter length. By the way, she won the class with a very good score. She obviously was not going to use her handicap as an excuse to prevent her from pursuing her equestrian goals.

Some physical challenges involve coping with pain. Dressage trainer Pamela Goodrich — member of the United States squad at the World Championships in Toronto, Canada in 1986 and team gold medalist at the 1987 Olympic Festival in Raleigh, North Carolina — epitomizes toughness and courage in the face of great pain. For three years a degenerating arthritic hip took its toll. Her gait became badly distorted, her left side atrophied, and lines of pain were becoming etched in her face. Pam had a limp all right, but it was not a loser's limp. This dynamic woman never let her disability and consuming pain affect her, either on or off the horse. She continued to teach, train, and compete with no complaints or excuses. She stood on a box to mount and hobbled painfully away when she got off. Over the years she had to shorten her irons, particularly the left one, so that her thigh was almost parallel to the ground. Her hip angle would not open enough to allow her to sit on horses correctly. Yet this distortion in her position never stopped her from schooling and riding effectively.

Doctors had explained to her that most artificial hips were strongest when first inserted and that over time they weakened. They also told her that the hip probably could only be replaced only once. So Pam chose to delay the operation as long as possible, feeling that she'd rather endure the pain than have the operation when she was still in her early 30s and end up in a wheelchair when she was 50.

Having made her decision, she had to learn to cope with the pain. She rationalized that her pain was not a warning that signaled rest.

Doing more or less work was not going to make her hip any better. So rather than be controlled by searing pain, she stayed busy with work-days that averaged 12 hours and taught herself to ride with an intense concentration that enabled her to block out her discomfort. Pam said, "I just kept my eye on my goals, which were riding and improving the horses."

Nights were more difficult. The pain was so intense that she could hardly sleep. And when she did sleep, the pain would wake her up if she rolled over.

Eventually, nature made the decision for her to have the hip re-placed: When the hip seized up so much that she physically couldn't ride anymore, it was time. She had the operation, and the doctors were amazed by the speed of her recovery. I was not amazed. I had experienced firsthand the determination and strength of will of this woman who refused to let relentless pain stop her.

Pam Goodrich had a limp all right, but it was not a loser's limp

Don't tell Nicole Uphoff that at the tender age of 21 she was too young and inexperienced to win the Gold Medal in dressage at the Seoul Olympics

Overcoming Other Obstacles

So you don't have any physical defects. Then what's *your* loser's limp? Are you too young? Or too old? Well, don't tell Germany's Nicole Uphoff that at the tender age of 21 she was too young and inexperienced to win the Gold Medal in dressage at the 1988 Olympics in Seoul, Korea. And be sure not to tell Bill Roycroft that while in his 60's he was too old to compete on the Australian Three Day team at the 1976 Olympics held at Bromont, Quebec.

Perhaps you are just fine. You are fit and healthy and in your prime. It's your horse's shortcomings that provide you with a number of ready-made excuses.

How would you like to compete seriously in dressage with the big warmbloods while you're riding a 14.3-hand horse (almost a pony)? That was the situation for Lendon Gray, veteran of the 1978 World Championships and the 1980 and 1988 Olympic teams. Lendon and Seldom Seen were scoffed at and discouraged throughout their long and successful career. People doubted she could train a small Connemara/Thoroughbred to the highest level in dressage. Not only did she accomplish that but she was competitive enough to win National Championships every year. After such successes, the next logical step for this pair would be to represent the United States in European competition. The people who had to choose the team were concerned. They felt that the United States would get laughed out of Europe for allowing a near-pony to compete internationally. Their answer was to measure him again, hoping desperately that he had shrunk an inch — which would make him ineligible for competition. Lendon received little support for her international ambitions.

So what did she do? She solicited a number of friends and fans to send her to Europe. As a result, Seldom Seen competed successfully at many other big shows, placing well against top European competition. It was touching to see a videotape of an awards ceremony in Europe with all the large warmbloods galloping along nose to tail; then after a space of about 30 meters, here comes the diminutive champion, Seldom Seen! There were many stages throughout the "pony's" career when Lendon could have listened to all the discouraging talk. But she believed in her horse, did not use his size as a loser's limp, and went on to become one of the dressage world's most memorable success stories.

Maybe you don't have international aspirations. Perhaps your situation is more similar to Jean Sangdahl's. Jean is an amateur dressage rider whose prospect was a sweet but very lazy quarter horse, Tancredi. "Credi" was not a terrific mover and the consensus was that Jean would be lucky if she could train this "limited" horse even through Second Level. But Jean was not discouraged. This dedicated rider labored diligently under supervision and successfully schooled her horse through all the Grand Prix movements. As it turned out

Despite all the discouraging talk, Lendon Gray did not use her small horse's size as a loser's limp — and went on to become one of the dressage world's most memorable success stories

"Credi" showed particular talent for the two most difficult movements, piaffe and passage. How fortunate that Jean refused to see her horse's physical shortcomings as an excuse to settle for less. Because she wouldn't perceive her horse as limited, "Credi" developed well beyond the athletic ability he was given by nature.

Not having enough time is another common excuse. Perhaps you have a job, a family, children, animals, and various other commitments. Somehow there is little time and energy left for your horse. You would love to devote consistent time to your riding. But how can you ever improve when you are being pulled in so many directions?

My friend Tacie epitomizes the words "enthusiastic" and "effervescent." She could easily have a long list of ready-made excuses for not finding the time to ride. She and her husband recently started a vineyard, and any new business demands time and attention. Tacie is out there daily on her hands and knees tying vines, pruning, and picking. In addition, she raises three children all under the age of five and cares for many various farm critters.

Yet she never uses her commitments as an excuse. In fact she feels that since she does so many things for others, riding is the one thing she can do for her *own* well-being. Making time for her riding is what keeps her sane. To manage, she gets up at five a.m. While driving to the barn, she visualizes a blackboard (like the one discussed on p. 51). Her blackboard has all the hassles and demands of the day written on it. She mentally takes an eraser and wipes the slate clean. By doing so, she's free to concentrate on her riding. Giving this time to herself is what enables her to give so much to everyone else around her. In Tacie's words, "When you are one with your horse, it is the ultimate high. One fabulous shoulder-in or extended trot, and I can conquer anything that comes my way for the rest of the day."

In addition, Tacie's advice for those who would use lack of support as another excuse is to invite your family or significant other to a competition. When they see how much fun you have and how you put your whole heart into it, it will turn them around. Explain to your family what this sport means to you. It is therapeutic. It is your release. It is something you do for yourself so you can give happily to them. If they still do not catch your enthusiasm, make a trade-off: I will support your golf, skiing, or football, if you will support my riding.

What if you live in an area where instruction is not readily available? Or perhaps you cannot afford the help. So what? During the first four years of my dressage career, I probably had a total of twelve lessons. My budget could only handle two two-day clinics per year. My instructor, Cindy Sydnor, often got her fee in spare change from

It's really fun to watch Jane Hamlin transform '90-pound weaklings'
into strong, graceful athletes

my waitressing tips. You can be sure I absorbed everything I possibly could from those precious but infrequent sessions and faithfully did my homework. In between, I supplemented my education by reading everything I could get my hands on, auditing clinics, and using the comments from judges as additional lessons. Progress was slow, but my horse and I did improve. *It's not what you don't have that matters. It's what you do with what you have.*

Jane Hamlin, head trainer at Huntington Farm in South Strafford, Vermont, knows this all too well. Like many of us, she does not have the resources to buy fancy horses. What a terrific excuse for not succeeding! Jane, however, enjoys the challenge of creating "silk purses from sow's ears." Because her bank account is modest, she buys inexpensive horses and works her magic. She finds many of these horses as rejects from the racetrack. They come to Jane thin, nervous, and uneducated. They leave muscled, secure, and obedient. Jane has the special knack of looking at weedy horses and visualizing what they can *become*. She usually warns me not to laugh the first time I see her new prospect. During the ensuing months, her refrain is usually, "You just wait. I believe in this horse." It's really fun to watch her transform these "90-pound weaklings" into strong, graceful athletes. As it should be, her sense of accomplishment is just as great as someone's who buys an expensive horse and does well on the A Circuit. Jane's finances are incidental. She could easily use this deficiency as a convenient excuse — just as the others discussed earlier could use their personal problems as reasons to fail. But instead they have all chosen to succeed. How about you? Abandon your loser's limp, commit yourself to your dream, and work diligently to realize your goals.

Part Two

TRAINING

Art ends where violence begins.
Violence begins where knowledge ends.
— Anonymous

5

Behavior Modification

Whether or not by choice, most of us are thrust into the role of trainer. Even if we depend on lessons and clinics for instruction, we take the responsibility of teaching our horses between those sessions. The training might be as basic as requiring obedience, or as sophisticated as schooling piaffe. In any case, the successful trainer needs a clear method to be able to communicate effectively with his horse.

To do this, you should become familiar with the theory of behavior modification. To shape behavior, *you* provide a stimulus, your *horse* provides the response, and *you* reward or punish his response (diagram I). Reward encourages repetition of the response. Punishment discourages the response. Through this process you begin to develop a nonverbal language, a method to communicate. The technique is the same whether you are training a hunter, jumper, reining horse, dressage horse, or pleasure horse.

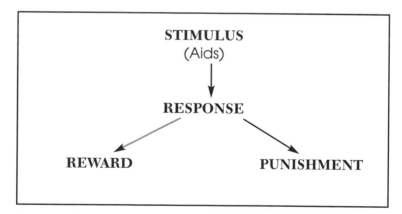

Diagram I. To shape behavior, you provide a stimulus, your horse provides a response, and you reward or punish his response

The Stimulus

Consistency of Aids

Consistency is vital to training and shaping behavior. Be consistent both when you apply aids as well as when you reward or punish the response. If you train with inconsistency, progress will be slow and your horse will be frequently confused or frustrated.

If your aids are consistent, however, your horse will not have to guess what you mean by a particular signal. One aid should mean one and only one thing. When you want to communicate something else, you should have a totally different aid. There are so many possible combinations of seat, leg, and hand that your language can be very specific. The young horse learns a simple and limited vocabulary (stop, go, turn right, turn left). The advanced horse has quite an extensive vocabulary that has been developed one signal at a time. You teach those signals by applying the aid exactly the same way each time, getting the desired response, then praising lavishly.

Theoretically you can train your horse to respond to any aid as long as you follow this method of shaping behavior. Let's say you decide to employ an unorthodox signal such as using your hand to touch the horse on his left shoulder to ask for the left-lead canter. This stimulus, or aid, is your hand on the horse's shoulder. Since your horse is not educated to the touch of your hand, elicit a response by combining the touch with a gentle kick, a tap with the whip, a voice command—or all of the above. As a result, your horse responds to the stimulus. If he responds incorrectly—ignores you, trots faster, or picks up the wrong lead—start again and *repeat* the aid (punishment). When he finally picks up the left lead, reward by praising generously. Once he understands, eliminate the whip, kick, or voice, and he should canter from the hand aid only (diagram II).

When training, it is helpful to be clear about which parts of *your* body control which parts of the horse's body. Trainer Pamela Goodrich breaks this down as shown in diagram III.

Having a guideline like this is useful because sometimes *we* get rewarded by the horse for using the wrong aids. As a result, we develop an incorrect conditioned response. An example of this would be when you ask for a downward transition by pulling on the reins. This can get you from one gait to the next, so you are being rewarded for pulling on the reins. However, by pulling on the reins you also stop the hind legs.

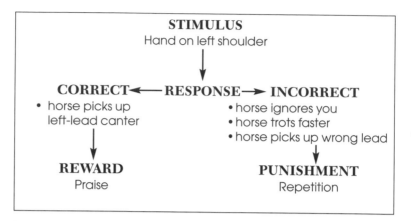

Diagram II. Sequence of events when using behavior modification to teach the horse a hand signal for left-lead canter

You get from canter to trot or from trot to walk, but you interfere with the forward movement of the hind legs (fig. 18). The sequence becomes: stop the hind legs, the back goes down, and the head comes up. You've achieved your transition, but now you have to reconnect your horse. On the other hand, if you had trained your horse to your back and used your back rather than your hands, you could have done the transition and at the same time left the hind legs free to keep coming forward.

SEAT + BACK	
• Rhythm • Length of stride • Suspension	• Downward transitions • Position of the horse's body

LEGS	
• Forward movement • Engagement	• Position of the hind legs

REINS	
• Flexion (left, right, in) • Height of the neck • Length of the neck	• Receiving forward energy of the hind legs • Position of the forehand

Diagram III. In order to avoid getting positively reinforced by the horse for using the wrong aids, it is helpful to be clear about which parts of your body control which parts of the horse's body

*18   By pulling on the reins you get from trot to walk, but
you interfere with the forward movement of the hind legs*

Another example is when a rider uses the wrong part of his body to correct a frequent error in the shoulder-in. When the horse's shoulders are brought in, the animal drifts off the track to avoid the engagement of the inside hind leg. Instinct encourages the rider to bring his hands to the wall to keep the horse from drifting in. The rider is rewarded for using the reins to fix the drift as the horse stays on the track. But he ends up with a "head-and-neck-in" rather than a shoulder-in, and there is no engagement of the inner hind leg (fig. 19).

By realizing that the problem lies with the inner hind leg stepping wide, diagram III tells the rider to fix the drift with his own inside leg. This is because the rider's leg commands the corresponding hind leg.

Use diagram III to avoid common mistakes like the ones described. Just figure out which part of the horse's body needs to be addressed and use the appropriate part of your body. Initially, it'll take some thought and discipline. Eventually, it becomes automatic.

*19   The rider brings his hands to the wall to keep
the horse from drifting in. . . . He ends up with a
"head-and-neck-in" rather than a shoulder-in*

Analyzing Movements

Prior to riding, you can also train yourself to be consistent by learning the aids for every movement you do with your horse. You can do
this in the comfort of your own living room. To begin, it might be helpful for you to write them out. To be sure your priorities are right, go
through the aids by always describing the seat first, followed by the legs
and lastly the hands. Say aloud or even write down the position of each
seat bone, leg, and hand and whether the aid is active or passive. If the
aid is active, describe the particular action. Books such as *The
Complete Training of Horse and Rider* by Alois Podhajsky and my own
Cross-Train Your Horse and *More Cross-Training* give precise aids for
each movement.

Here's an example of this procedure of learning the aids at home.

Exercise: Leg yield to the right (away from the left leg):
- Seat: sit squarely and balanced over the middle of your horse.
- Right leg: on the girth for forward movement.
- Left leg: behind the girth for sideways movement. Both legs are passive unless the horse needs to be sent either more forward or more sideways. In that case, the appropriate leg squeezes and releases.
- Left rein: vibrates for flexion at the poll.
- Right rein: steady and supporting to keep the neck straight.

To be precise you need to be thoroughly familiar with the aids for everything you do. If you're not clear, at least mentally, how can you expect your horse to be? At first this process is time consuming, since you must go through each exercise step by step in your mind. It's similar to learning a foreign language (which is essentially what you are doing). In the beginning, you hear the unfamiliar words and have to go through the step of translating then in your head; in time you understand the foreign words without having to translate.

Your thinking and riding will be a bit mechanical at this point, but it is a temporary stage. Eventually you develop a feel for the movement.

Reward and Punishment

Once you have given a stimulus (the aid) and your horse responds, you must react to the response. You establish behavior in this way. Reward encourages the behavior to be repeated. Punishment discourages a behavior.

Reward

The trainer who desires a happy horse and a harmonious partnership focuses more on reward than punishment. What kinds of things can you do to reward?

- A pat on the neck or scratch at the withers
- Verbal praise—"Good Boy!" or "Good Girl!"
- Take a break—a walk on a loose rein

- Treats such as sugar or carrots to be given occasionally when teaching something particularly difficult or trauma-producing
- Finish the session. If you horse has learned something new or tried particularly hard, reward by ending the work. Get off and put him away even after a very short session. Or perhaps go for a relaxing hack. As with all reward, this will encourage him to repeat his response the next time.

Many riders incorrectly perceive the finish of an aid as the horse's reward. When you use your seat, legs, or reins, consider the relaxation of the aid as *part* of the aid rather than a reward (e.g., squeeze/release constitutes the aid itself).

Punishment

Starting from the least severe, what kinds of things are used to punish?

a. Absence of reward
b. Repetition of an exercise
c. Strong aids

a. Absence of reward is punishment. When teaching a new signal or a new movement, it's vital to reward every time you give the aid and receive a better or a correct response. You don't have to make a big fuss, but acknowledge his efforts with a pat or a clear "Good Boy." During this time, when forming a new habit, the absence of reward is virtually the same as punishment. If you fail to reward, you'll cancel the very behavior you want.

Absence of punishment is *not* reward. If you think it is, and you school with that approach, chances are your horse will be unhappy and mechanical.

Forming a partnership that is beautiful—two bodies/one mind—starts with mutual respect and a willingness to show appreciation for efforts. After all, you are the one with the desire to ride. Your horse would probably rather be eating or out in a field with his buddies. You must create desire for him. The horse's motivation doesn't come from within, as with a human being. He does what he does for you, and only because you ask. The least you can do is reward him for his cooperation so that he is happy in his work and eager to please.

b. Repetition of an exercise is a mild form of punishment. Let's say you ride a ten-meter circle and your horse doesn't bend properly. A gentle punishment is to stay on that circle. How long you stay on it depends on whether or not ten-meter circles are already in his repertoire. With the horse who has already shown his ability to do a ten-meter circle bending correctly, you stay there until it is quite good.

With the green or laterally stiff horse, you repeat the circle until he bends a little better. A shade better is good enough for this horse and earns him a reward. If you see progress only in black or white (i.e., it's either awful or it's perfect), you won't be generous enough with a reward. As a result both you and your horse will be frustrated.

If you learn to be satisfied with progress in small increments, your training sessions will be happier for both you and your horse. One degree better and another degree better and another degree better soon becomes many degrees better. If you expect things to get a whole lot better in one day, you are being unrealistic—you will get tight or lose your temper, and the effects will show in your horse.

I once gave a frustrated rider an exercise to improve her canter departs. There was some immediate improvement, and I was quite satisfied. The rider, however, wasn't happy with just a little bit better. Rather than being justifiably pleased, she was still frustrated. The horse was unhappy, too, since without reward he had no way of knowing that he was doing better. The rider thought she'd have the perfect canter depart after doing this exercise a couple of times. What a sad and negative way to train and learn.

c. Occasionally you will need to punish with strong aids. Strong aids include the sharp or aggressive use of whip, legs, or hands. They are appropriate when you are dealing with disobediences. By disobediences I refer to a horse's uncooperative behavior as having a mental origin—an unwillingness or lack of submission—as opposed to physical difficulties. However, sometimes a horse's behavior is perceived as a disobedience when, in fact, his actions may stem from other causes. It's important to recognize these other causes because in such cases strong aids should not be used. They include things like:

1. **Your aid is unclear or interferes with the horse**

2. **The horse's body is not in a position to be obedient**

3. **The horse is not strong enough to do the exercise**

4. **Tension**

5. **Pain**

1. If your aids are unclear, your horse can't be expected to understand what you're asking. First, you must be clear about the aids mentally. Then, you must be steady and controlled enough in your position so that your horse doesn't have to sort through your extraneous motion to feel the aid. For example, you ask for a half-pass in the trot and your horse keeps breaking into a canter. He feels your outside leg behind the girth and tries to be obedient, so he canters. If your aids had been clear, you should have:

- Differentiated between a leg that quickly brushes back to ask for a canter depart, and one that stays back to ask him to go sideways
- Initiated the sideways motion with your body weight by stepping down into the inside iron and using your outside rein (rather than just pushing him sideways with your outside leg)

In addition, your aids must not interfere with your horse. Let's say you ask for a flying change and your horse changes first with the hind legs and one stride later he changes in front. The change is not clean, but not as the result of disobedience. If you didn't soften your new inside hand forward in the moment of the change, the hand blocks the horse and makes it difficult for him to switch in front.

2. If the horse's body is not in a position to do the exercise, he should not be punished for disobediences. For example, you want your horse to leg yield, and rather than asking for flexion at the poll, your inside hand is too strong and your outside rein is not supporting—so you end up with the neck bent. The degree to which the neck is cranked around is the degree to which the horse does not cross behind. As the neck is straightened, the horse's body will be in a better position to cross behind and do a good leg yield.

3. If your horse is learning a new exercise, and he's "disobedient" simply because he's not strong enough yet to perform it, find ways to take the difficulty out of the exercise rather than punishing him. Let's say you've decided to do a shoulder-in at the trot down the long side of the arena and your horse is not cooperating. Here are some things you can do to take the difficulty out of the exercise until he becomes strong enough to do it easily.

- Walk rather than trot
- Ask for less angle
- Ask for fewer steps

4. Sometimes horses appear disobedient because they're tense. Their tension causes them to anticipate what they *think* you want. In this case, quietly repeat your request rather than punishing. There's already tension involved in trying too hard, and you will create even more tension if you punish the worried horse.

Or maybe your horse expresses his tension by shying. If he shies at a genuinely scary object and you punish him, you'll add to his apprehension and he'll be even more afraid. A better alternative would be to position his head and neck away from the object in order to direct his focus elsewhere; then ride by it, and while you are adjacent to it, soften your hands to alleviate some of the tension that has been built up (fig. 20).

20   If your horse shies at something genuinely scary, position his head and neck away from the object in order to direct his focus elsewhere

5. More often than we realize, disobedience has its roots in pain. Horses by nature are gentle and kind and eager to please. So if you find yourself dealing with a behavioral problem, you might explore the possibility that the disobedience is from pain rather than belligerence. I remember a horse who started throwing his head when asked to do something as simple as bend. The horse was basically a cooperative sort and this behavior was not typical for him. So his owner called the veterinarian. As it turned out, he had an extremely painful tooth that caused him to react to even gentle pressure on the reins.

I also recall a horse who had been fairly simple to break, but over time became progressively more difficult to mount. Eventually, whenever the rider settled into the saddle, the horse would erupt into fits of bucking. It was later discovered by an equine masseuse that this horse had developed a very sore back as the result of an ill-fitting saddle and simply could not tolerate the rider's weight.

A friend of mine owned a young horse who was branded a rogue by several top trainers because he was a chronic rearer. His behavior was considered a discipline problem and was treated accordingly. This approach didn't work, and things deteriorated. Luckily, a chiropractor discovered three vertebrae severely out of line. Once the alignment was corrected (with the same kind of adjustment a chiropractor would make on a human spine), my friend found herself dealing with a totally different animal.

So remember that our horses do talk in their own way. We just need to be sensitive enough to understand their language and hear what they are saying. Give the "rogue" the benefit of the doubt. Search for physical sources of discomfort. Do what you can to alleviate the problem (massage, drugs, etc.) and then see if you are in fact dealing with a disobedience.

When you've decided that punishment is appropriate, remember how horses learn. They learn by immediate association. People think deductively. Horses do not. In order to get your point across, you must make a decision and act upon it quickly. If you've asked your horse to move away from your leg and he doesn't, don't wait to react. As soon as you've given an aid that's been ignored, immediately get after him with the whip in a way that sends him sideways. Otherwise, too much time passes for him to associate his action (or inaction) with what you're punishing him for. Your aid and the reward or punishment must be done quickly in order to take advantage of the way a horse learns. Once your aid is given, every stride he takes without going sideways tells him that *sometimes* it's okay to ignore you.

Punishment can be strong, but should always be done in a calculated manner. Punish with a purpose—to educate. Never punish because you're emotionally upset or out of control.

Punishment can be strong, but is not unjust as long as the reward is equally strong. In the above example, if you've had to use the whip aggressively to get your horse to move away from your leg, be sure to praise with equal enthusiasm when he is obedient. Punishment is rarely resented when subsequent efforts are rewarded.

One Practical Application of Behavior Modification

Now that you're familiar with behavior modification, let's use it in training. I've chosen, as our example, *putting the horse in front of the leg*. This requires the horse to go forward willingly from light aids—a desirable goal for riders in every riding discipline.

Have you ever heard yourself say that a particular horse needs a lot of leg, or that you're just not strong enough to make him go forward? To be sure, you want to be strong enough to control your legs so that they can remain quietly on your horse's side. But you shouldn't need brute strength to be able to give aids. After all, you don't *make* a large animal go forward or sideways or lengthen his stride. You *ask* him to do these things by giving him an aid as a signal.

If you need to use strength to create forward movement, your horse has *you* very well trained. The process probably began innocently enough when you lightly closed your legs to ask your horse to go forward. When he didn't, you pressed harder. He responded a little, so you were rewarded for squeezing harder. The next time you did even more. Over time, your horse gets more dull. So you do even more, end up getting tired, and find you need to give him a break. Before you know it, he has you perfectly trained!

If this sounds familiar, then you need to put your horse in front of the leg. You'll have to go through the process of resensitizing him to your leg. Perhaps your horse is fifteen years old and has been dull for such a long time that you think he'll never respond to light aids. Well, just watch what he does on a summer's day when the flies are out. All a fly has to do is land on his side, and he flicks it off with his tail. Now if your thick-skinned friend is sensitive enough to feel a fly on his side, then he ought to be able to feel subtle leg aids if he's properly schooled to respond to them.

Why should you bother to go through this resensitizing process? Several reasons. A beautifully-trained horse "gives the impression of doing of his own accord what is required of him."[1] This is impossible if your aids are visible. Also, if your aids are too strong, you distort your position.

You therefore become less effective as well as less elegant. In addition, one of your training goals is to make your horse more pleasurable to ride. If you're exhausted because you feel like you've spent 45 minutes on an abductor/adductor fitness machine (inner/outer thigh), your ride isn't much fun.

Convinced? Good. Let's go through the process of putting your horse in front of the leg. We use basic behavior-modification principles. As discussed earlier, you give a stimulus, which is followed by your horse's response (or lack of one), and then you either reward or punish. Reward encourages a behavior to be repeated. Punishment discourages a behavior.

- Start by vowing not to use leg aids that are strong, visible, or repetitive. Keep reminding yourself that a horse is very sensitive to touch. Remember that he can feel a fly. The rule is that you give just one aid. It is feather-light. And the response from your horse should be immediate and 100%.

- If the response is less—even 99.99%—take your whip and use it vigorously until you send your horse eagerly forward. It's important that you don't end the sensitizing process here. If you do, all you've accomplished is to sensitize your horse to the whip. You still haven't taught him anything about the leg.

- The important part of the process is to go back to exactly what you were trying to do and ask again with your feather-light aid.

- If the response is still not 100%, repeat the whole process. If you hear yourself saying things like, "that was better" or "pretty good," you still don't have 100%. What is "pretty good" inevitably becomes dull and behind the leg again. When you finally get the 100% wholeheartedly forward response to your feather-light aid, praise the horse a lot (see p. 73).

If you follow this system, you will soon have a horse that responds to light aids.

Since this book discusses training from a positive point of view, you might think the above process of resensitization is unduly harsh because you may have to use your whip quite aggressively initially. However, it is kinder to the horse to make your point, get it over with, and ultimately have an animal that responds to light, pleasant aids. This is preferable to constantly squeezing his sides or jabbing at him with big spurs. He will be a happier horse in the long run.

Two important things to remember:

- Every second you are on your horse you are either training or untraining. So be consistent. It's unfair to insist that your horse be in front of the leg when you're working and then, when you take a break or go on a hack, you go back to using strong, dull prolonged aids. Don't undo what you've just accomplished by being inconsistent. There are many gray areas in training, but forward is not one of them. Your horse is either 100% in front of the leg or he's not forward enough.

- If your horse is afraid of the whip or bucks dangerously when it's used, you can go through this process without one. After all, your goal is not to terrorize the animal or to get bucked off. So to punish for a less than 100% response, remove leg contact by taking them off his sides and kick vigorously until he goes enthusiastically forward (fig. 21). Then retest with your feather-light aid. If you use your legs instead of a whip, be sure there's a huge difference between the aid and the kicking. If you nudge and/or squeeze in order to punish, your horse could mistake that simply as a stronger aid, and you'll therefore be rewarding his dullness.

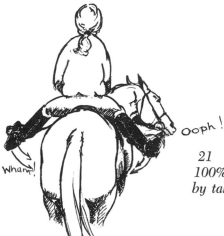

Ooph!

Wham!

21 To punish for a less than 100% response, remove contact by taking your legs off his sides and kick vigorously

6

Applying Your WIN Mechanism

Once you have a clear-cut, organized system for training, you can enhance your program by incorporating the skills you learned in Part One of the book. Let's see how you can use psychocybernetics, the power of positive speech, and the *As If* Principle to improve schooling.

Using Psychocybernetics

Psychocybernetic theory states that your subconscious mind believes everything you tell it and works relentlessly to accomplish your goals. You program yourself through vivid mental images and words.

Let's discuss those mental images first. The more vividly you image your goal, the more readily you create what you desire. Improve your visualization skills by starting at home, where you can build your images while in a relaxed state, free from distractions and external stimuli, such as your horse or other riders (see p. 18). Practice seeing your horse as you would like him to be.

Maybe you see him jumping a course fluidly—maintaining a good canter rhythm and length of stride for what the course demands and meeting each fence at a comfortable distance. Or perhaps you see him working consistently and quietly on the bit. Fill in the details as you create your image. Use all of your senses. If your horse has a crooked blaze on his face, *see* it. If you have difficulty filling in this detail, go to the stable and look at your horse. Then turn away or close your eyes and see if you can still see his blaze in your mind's eye. Repeat the process until it's easy for you to conjure up the image of his unique markings. *Hear* the even spacing of the steps of each stride for each gait. Is that difficult for you to imagine? Then listen to a real horse walking, trotting, and cantering on fairly firm footing. Close your eyes and listen. Then walk away and re-create the sound in your mind. If it is still difficult, go back and listen again. *Feel* the motion of your horse's movement and the shape of your saddle under your seat. Experience it and then recreate the feeling in your imagination when you are off the horse.

If you still have difficulty conjuring up your mental pictures, study videotapes of either yourself or someone else riding as you would like to ride. If your image fades, replay the tape as needed for a quick refresher. I went through a period when I would repeatedly watch an eight-second segment of Margit Otto-Crepin, international dressage champion from France, riding Corlandus in a collected trot. I would study them trotting through the short side of the arena. The collected trot showed unbelievable expression and self-carriage—it was very exciting to watch. I would play and rewind that section over and over until I could see Corlandus clearly in my mind.

When you see the power and expression of a horse like Corlandus, as ridden here by Margit Otto-Crepin, you can conjure up this image in your mind—and your own horse's gaits will become loftier and more beautiful by the day

After practicing your visualization skills at home, you can begin to bring the images to your actual schooling sessions. Sometimes, when schooling, I "ride" Corlandus, and my own horse's trot becomes loftier and more beautiful by the day. Or in my mind's eye I see myself and my horse doing the perfect half-pass or canter serpentine. By visualizing the frame, the balance, and my horse's calm submission while executing these particularly difficult movements or exercises with textbook perfection, I ride better and the horse in turn responds.

Other times when riding, I visualize parts of the horse. Certain parts often reflect what is going on in the rest of the horse. For example, with a horse that is tense in the walk, I focus on his eye. I picture it staying calm and soft (fig. 22). I tenaciously hold onto that image through the walk work and I invariably experience a vast reduction in the level of tension.

22 *Visualize parts of the horse that reflect
what is going on in the rest of his body.
For example, focus on his eye —
picture it staying calm and soft*

With a nervous horse that opens his mouth, crosses his jaw, and/or drops the bit, I will focus on his mouth. In my mind the mouth remains quietly closed.

In downward transitions from extensions, the part of the body I zero in on is the horse's shoulders. I watch those shoulders rise up in front of me, rather than seeing them sink away—which is what happens when the transition is being done on the forehand.

With a horse that scurries over the top of a jump, concentrate on his back and neck. Think of a "snapshot moment" in the air and picture him stretching in an arc through his back and down with his neck.

Visualization skills will add an exciting dimension to your regular training sessions. Most important is that by programming your mind, in time you will experience some very positive, tangible results in your riding. Additionally, you will develop the ability to stay focused. You'll feel your powers of concentration grow as you are eventually able to hold on to your images throughout a ride in spite of distractions. Since most riding is so cerebral, this is an invaluable skill.

Another by-product of all this work is that you will become less anxious in your riding. It's impossible to think about two things at once. In other words, you can't be worried about how your horse usually goes or what he *might* do, if you are intensely focused on creating and sustaining your positive images.

Applying the Power of Positive Speech

In Part One we discussed the power of words. What you say is what you get. By repeating words like "harmony," "powerful," "elegance," and "joyful," you can influence the quality of your ride. These words evoke strong feelings and images, and the words are all heard by your subconscious. Remember, your mind believes everything you say and will do its best to help you achieve what it perceives as your goal. So be sure you don't inadvertently tell yourself that you're a klutz and that you don't look graceful and coordinated on your horse. Or don't tell yourself that you'll probably stop in the middle of the triple combination—because that's exactly what will happen!

You can also take advantage of the power of positive speech by using your favorite word like a Hindu mantra. The repeated chanting of a particular word can have a soothing effect on you and consequently on your horse. Repeating your mantra serves as a form of self-hypnosis—a very desirable condition, since hypnosis reflects a state of deep relaxation.

While riding a horse who struggled doing trot half-passes and became irregular in his rhythm, I would silently chant "rhy-thm, rhy-thm" in the regular rhythm of the trot to help us both.

Along the same lines, you can repeat "1-2-3, 1-2-3" to help steady your horse's rhythm while jumping a stadium or hunter course.

Or how about, at the beginning of your session, silently repeating the word "calm" or "confident" to get yourself focused and concentrated as well as relaxed.

The possibilities are endless. Be creative. Find a mantra that suits your needs and take advantage of the awesome power of positive speech.

Incorporating the *As If* Principle in Training

Remember the *As If* Principle? If you want to possess a quality, act "as if" you already do, and it'll soon become yours. Well, how about applying this principle to your training?

World Championship event rider Kim Walnes is a great advocate of the *As If* Principle. She claims that the idea is not to school in a reactive state. Don't react to what your horse is offering, but ride each movement "as if" he were perfect. Rather than reacting to his mental state or to his resistances, act "as if" he were calm and submissive and watch how he begins to mirror your attitude and body movement.

Kim also suggests acting "as if" you are a particular rider you truly admire. She says, "Become that rider. And since you are no longer you, you can remove your own limitations and act as that rider would act."

Go ahead, give it a shot. Act "as if" you're Virginia Leng, Christine Stuckelberger, or Michael Matz—and just watch how you and your horse improve.

7

The Positive Approach to Training Challenges

Resistance

I have discussed earlier (p. 74) how you handle *disobedience* through negative reinforcement. This chapter goes on to discuss coping with *resistance*. The American Horse Shows Association (AHSA) Rule Book explains the difference between disobedience and resistance in this way: "a horse may resist physically when responding to the rider's aids by showing a lack of suppleness in movements or transitions whereas disobedience involves willful escape." That is, a disobedient horse that is not *willing* to go forward might react by rearing or stopping at a jump and wheeling. A resistant horse might stiffen against the rider's hand during a transition or grab at the bit as he rushes to the jumps. Keep in mind, however, that one does not preclude the other; disobedience and resistance may overlap.

Resistance is inevitable in schooling, so it would be helpful to have a plan to deal with it and keep it to a minimum. You can keep resistance to a minimum by being systematic in your schooling. Over the long term, being systematic assumes that there is a thoughtful progression in the work so that the horse is not asked to do anything that he is not physically or mentally prepared to do.

Your long-range plan should be designed with the development of the horse in mind. As time goes on, he becomes progressively more supple, flexible, and strong. It would be disastrous to ask a young horse who is just comfortable doing 20-meter circles to suddenly do 6-meter circles—a figure appropriate only for an older, more balanced horse. It would make more sense to develop flexibility by next doing 15-meter circles. When he can easily bend along that arc in both directions, you then decrease to 12 meters, then 10 meters, then 8 meters, and finally 6 meters. This progression occurs over months, or more likely years, depending on the horse.

If you abruptly went from 20 meters to 6 meters, perhaps you'd be lucky enough that your horse would resist sufficiently for you to realize he is not physically ready. Unfortunately, what often happens is that rather than violently or obviously resisting, your horse evades the difficulty of the exercise in subtle ways. In this case, he might react to the demands of the increased bending by swinging his hindquarters slightly out (fig. 23). Such *evasions* are potentially more dangerous than resistances because their subtlety allows them to creep in unnoticed by the rider and become firmly established. Resistances, on the other hand, are so obvious that they are hard to miss.

Having a ground person or instructor watching makes it simpler for you to deal with evasions as they occur in a normal schooling situation. Your ground person becomes your eyes. However, if you spend much of the time on your own, you can ensure against evasions in the form of sound, methodical planning. A helpful step in this direction is to obtain a booklet of the AHSA dressage tests and read what is included at each level. These tests are designed with the systematic development of the horse in mind. As such, the lower-level tests can be useful for riders engaged in disciplines other than dressage. Learn what is contained in each level as well as what additional movements are introduced. This gives you a rough guideline for long-term planning (diagram IV).

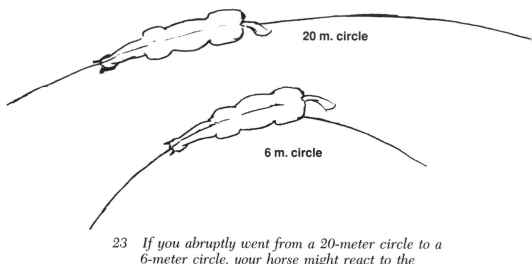

20 m. circle

6 m. circle

23 *If you abruptly went from a 20-meter circle to a*
6-meter circle, your horse might react to the
demands of the increased bending by swinging
his hindquarters slightly out

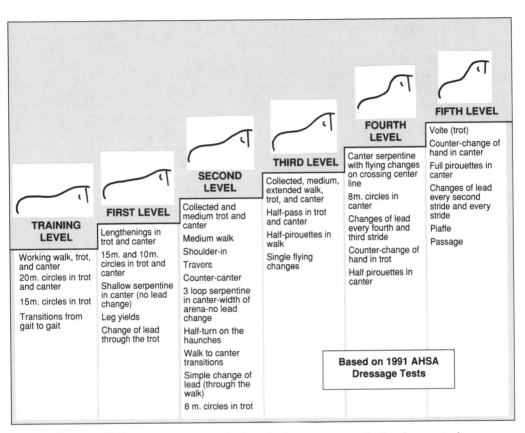

TRAINING LEVEL	FIRST LEVEL	SECOND LEVEL	THIRD LEVEL	FOURTH LEVEL	FIFTH LEVEL
Working walk, trot, and canter	Lengthenings in trot and canter	Collected and medium trot and canter	Collected, medium, extended walk, trot, and canter	Canter serpentine with flying changes on crossing center line	Volte (trot)
20m. circles in trot and canter	15m. and 10m. circles in trot and canter	Medium walk	Half-pass in trot and canter	8m. circles in canter	Counter-change of hand in canter
15m. circles in trot	Shallow serpentine in canter (no lead change)	Shoulder-in	Half-pirouettes in walk	Changes of lead every fourth and third stride	Full pirouettes in canter
Transitions from gait to gait	Leg yields	Travers	Single flying changes	Counter-change of hand in trot	Changes of lead every second stride and every stride
	Change of lead through the trot	Counter-canter		Half pirouettes in canter	Piaffe
		3 loop serpentine in canter-width of arena-no lead change			Passage
		Half-turn on the haunches			
		Walk to canter transitions			
		Simple change of lead (through the walk)		**Based on 1991 AHSA Dressage Tests**	
		8 m. circles in trot			

Diagram IV. Dressage tests are designed with the systematic development of the horse in mind and can therefore be used as guidelines for training

Along the same lines, follow a systematic progression of training for the horse who jumps. First, the horse should be asked to negotiate trotting poles (a series of poles on the ground set at a distance of 4 to 4½ feet apart). Then he can be asked to trot and eventually canter rails on the ground as a course. Next, incorporate gymnastic lines at the trot, and later the canter, into schooling. Gymnastic lines consist of a series of fences built to improve the horse's ability to rock back on his hocks and jump. They help make the horse more cat-like and agile so that he can cleverly cope with difficult things such as odd striding distances when they occur. When this foundation has been laid, you can begin to canter courses — increasing the size of the jumps as the schooling continues.

LEVELS OF COMPETITION FOR HORSE TRIALS

NOVICE	TRAINING	PRELIMINARY	INTERMEDIATE	ADVANCED
THE DRESSAGE TEST				
Includes working gaits with all work done down the long side, across the diagonal or on a 20m. circle.	Includes 15m. circles and lengthening at the walk and trot.	Requires lengthening at all three gaits. Can include leg-yielding and shoulder-in and 10m. circles.	Introduces medium trot, plus walk to canter transitions and counter canter serpentines.	Requires 10m. circles, the half-pass, and all extensions.
THE CROSS-COUNTRY COURSE				
Straightforward, solid, simple obstacles with true ground lines. Only two obstacles in combination with a minimum of two strides (33 ft) between them. 2,000m. at 350-400 mpm with 12-20 jumping efforts.	Not too testing-a series of simple steps up or down or a simple table jump may be introduced. Combinations may include 2 or more jumping efforts with a minimum of 1 stride (22 ft) between obstacles-obstacles of several elements can be included but not corners or bounces. 2,500m. at 400-500 mpm with 16-22 jumping efforts.	May include moderate testing of lengthening and shortening of stride, of balance on sharper turns, of boldness and athletic ability. May contain a more substantial bank, a 2 or 3 stride sunken road, or a simple bounce. 2,000-3,000m. at 520 mpm with 18-26 jumping efforts.	Tests agility and boldness by introducing jumps with turns on slopes, water to water obstacles, bounces and options. 2,400-3,500m. at 520-550 mpm with 20-28 jumping efforts.	Demonstrate exceptional jumping ability, speed, courage, obedience, and suppleness. Galloping fences and turning to jump situations included. Water can include bounce entries and exits, and water to water. Drops and ditches frequently found. 3,250-4000m. at 570 mpm with 22-30 jumping efforts.
THE JUMPING COURSE				
Straight and spread obstacles and one combination with two jumping efforts. No false ground lines in cross-country or jumping. 400-500 m. at 300 mpm with 8-12 jumping efforts.	May include one double and one triple combination. No water jumps, slopes, or ramps. 400-500m. at 325 mpm with 10-12 jumping efforts.	Show ability to jump accurately and recover quickly. More difficult combinations and related distances. Doubles, triples, banks, water and dikes may be included. 400-500m. at 350 mpm with 10-15 jumping efforts.	Introduces slightly greater heights and spreads and courses requiring adjustment of stride and speed. 500-600m. at 375 mpm with 12-15 jumping efforts.	Introduces FEI heights, spreads, and speeds. May include a double and a triple, with changes of direction and various types of upright and spread obstacles. 500-600m. at 400 mpm with 12-15 jumping efforts.

Refer to AHSA Rules for Combined Training for maximum dimensions of obstacles at each level in relation to height, spread, drops, and water.

Diagram V. The AHSA Rules for Combined Training offer a guideline for appropriate sizes of obstacles and suitable speeds at each stage of training

Developing the horse in this methodical way can reduce resistances in jumping. For example, the horse who is inclined to rush is taught through the use of gymnastic lines to back off the jump rather than run through it. The rider can leave the reins alone and let the horse learn from the gymnastic line itself.

The AHSA also puts out a booklet entitled *Rules for Combined Training* which contains the levels of competition for eventing. It therefore offers a guideline for appropriate sizes of obstacles and suitable speeds at each successive stage of training (diagram V).

You also need to be prepared to deal with evasions and resistances in daily work so that your approach is positive rather than punishing. The question that will allow the thinking rider to deal with resistance in a positive way is, "How can I make it easier for my horse to do what I am asking?" And then, if your horse is still struggling, determine how to make your objective less demanding.

Perhaps your goal is to teach your horse to do a simple change of canter lead through the trot. The first time you attempt this, your horse breaks to the trot, runs through the bridle, and if he picks up the canter at all, he ends up going on the same lead. Sound familiar?

Let's analyze the causes of the problem. The horse might run off in the trot from tension, confusion, or anticipation. He picks up the same lead because he stays in position for that lead canter. How can we make this exercise easier?

Using the knowledge that horses tend to anticipate — particularly when the exercises are done in the same spot in the ring — we can devise an exercise for this particular problem where he anticipates being relaxed rather than running. We can also get him to anticipate putting his body in a position that will eventually allow us to pick up the correct new lead.

Many horses are more relaxed in the walk, and the rider also has more time to get organized. So follow the steps outlined below. (If you have the type of horse in whom tension builds at the walk, start in whichever gait he is most relaxed.)

a) Begin by walking back and forth across the diagonal.

b) Next, walk across the diagonal and upon reaching X execute a leg yield away from the new inner leg until you reach the wall. (Although a leg yield is generally done with the horse's body straight, in this case it would be helpful to leg yield with the new inner leg on the girth and get him to bend a little. The bend will make it easier to later position him for the change of lead.)

c) Do steps a) and b) in the trot.

d) Canter across the diagonal, trot at X, and leg yield in the trot until you reach the wall (fig. 24).

e) When he does step d) quietly, ask for the new lead after however many trot steps are needed to position him correctly for the new lead.

f) Gradually decrease the number of trot steps to three.

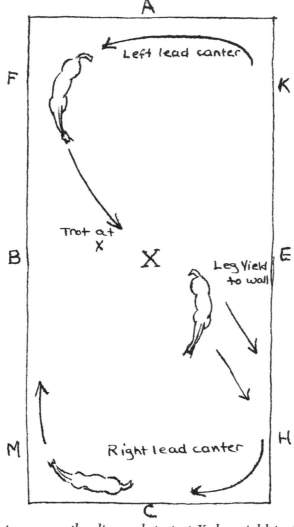

24   *Canter across the diagonal, trot at X, leg yield in the trot until you reach the wall, then ask for the new lead*

You might not be able to progress through all the steps in one day. You should advance only when each prior step is done quietly and in a relaxed manner. Your horse will let you know how many days you'll need to make it through all the steps until you reach your goal of a calm and balanced change of lead through the trot.

When you encounter resistance while jumping, think about how you can make it easier for the horse to do what you're asking. For instance, you find that your horse gets quick between two fences in a row. Take the difficulty out of the exercise by setting two fences 8 strides apart and keeping them quite small. And then relax your horse in the following way:

a) Trot to the first fence. Jump it. Halt quietly and reward. And then trot to and jump the second fence.

b) Canter and jump the first fence. Halt and reward. And then trot to and jump the second fence.

c) Now try cantering the line of fences in 8 strides. If your horse still rushes, go back and repeat steps a) and b).

This systematic method to keep resistance to a minimum can be applied to any riding problem. Decide what your end result is and ask yourself how to progressively make the exercise easier.

Despite the best-laid plans, you will still encounter resistance in training. Resistance is a very normal part of the training process. You should learn to accept its inevitability and not worry when you run into it. Worrying creates tension in the rider and consequently in the horse, making the resistance more difficult to resolve.

It's important to have a good attitude toward resistance. Don't panic when it happens—because many times some very positive results occur when you work through it. A resistance can give you an opportunity to practice and refine your riding skills (for example, if your horse never stops or looks at the jumps, then you won't know how to cope with the situation when it occurs; or if your horse never comes above the bit, you never get to practice putting him on the bit).

Get excited about the concept that the reason you're meeting with resistance is because you're progressing. You can probably ride your established first-level horse very easily at training and first level. However, as you increase your demands, you'll most likely have to contend with some form of opposition. We all tend to rebel when asked to leave our too-familiar comfort zones—and the horse is no exception. Look forward to working through the resistance and developing a stronger, better-balanced horse that you will be riding at second level.

Would you prefer to stagnate at the same level, or would you willingly leave your comfort zone and deal with the resistance in order to advance your horse's schooling? The latter, for sure. Leave the security of the schooling ring and go for a canter across a field. Or, instead of getting stuck in the hunter division, try some baby jumper or equitation classes, even if it is only at a schooling show.

In conclusion, don't be afraid of resistance. Get some good advice from a trainer who can help you evaluate why the horse is resisting or how he is evading your aids. A professional can give you a program for working through it. The rewards that lie beyond that layer of resistance are well worth the hassle.

Emotional Control

Frustration

The inevitable resistances that occur throughout training can lead to frustration. Frustration is normal, but your attitude towards handling it will determine whether it is a momentary inconvenience or whether it consumes you.

To deal with frustration over the long haul, get some perspective on your progress. Training should be thought of in terms of months and years, not days and weeks. When you feel like you are not making progress, recall a time from the past and ask yourself questions like, "What were my canter departs like three months ago?" "What did our lengthenings look like last year?" "Would my horse eagerly jump through water last season?" To get a sense of the progress that's been made, step back and look at the big picture. Remember when you were just trotting little fences. Or remember when your horse would refuse every coop he saw.

On a daily basis, plan to negate frustration by ending every session on a good note. Bring your horse back to the barn with both of you feeling satisfied. There will be times when you'll have to use your imagination to find something positive in the ride. Perhaps you'll have to finish with something very simple, such as a quiet walk-to-halt transition or a correctly executed 20-meter circle. Maybe you'll end your jumping session by jogging a cross-rail calmly and obediently. Or perhaps you'll finish your cross-country school by rhythmically galloping a simple ascending jump (an inviting ramp-like fence in which the front is lower than the back). Devise something that makes you feel a sense of rapport and accomplishment before putting your horse back in the barn.

You can make every session positive by not comparing your ride to the day before or what you *know* he can do. Instead, at the beginning of the ride, cruise around and evaluate what he has to offer you this day. How stiff does he feel? Is he calm and attentive or nervous and distracted? How does he feel in your hand? Evaluate. Then go about your various suppling exercises and movements to improve whatever is lacking. After a few minutes, re-evaluate, do the appropriate exercises again, and re-evaluate again. If you understand that progress is made in small increments, you will be satisfied with anything that is "a little bit better." Your horse will not go from lousy to perfect or from stiff to supple. He will get a little less lousy and a lot less lousy until he eventually becomes a little bit better, then a lot better. You're only setting yourself up for frustration if you evaluate your training sessions in terms of black and white. There are many shades of gray.

And if, in your heart, you truly believe that any small effort — anything that is a little better — is cause for celebration, you will *always* have a good ride. Maybe your satisfaction will even be based on your horse's finally standing still while being mounted. If you bring him back to the barn feeling that way, he will sense your satisfaction. Dissatisfaction only leads to your being frustrated, which in turn causes tension and anger. Tension and anger can result in a "me-against-him" atmosphere, rather than a spirit of cooperation.

During your schooling, remember again the shades of gray. Since repetition is the mildest form of punishment, repeat the appropriate exercise only until it is a little bit better and then reward by releasing the horse from the exercise. To expect instant results is unrealistic and discouraging. For example, imagine how difficult it is for a stiff horse to start bending — which is a basic flexibility exercise. Now suppose it's been years since you've touched your toes — also a flexibility exercise. When you tried, you could only reach as far as your knees. If someone forced you to touch your toes, you would feel pain and bodily resistance, and you'd probably hurt even more the next day. But if you allowed your body to become more flexible gradually, you would eventually touch your toes without any discomfort. Now empathize with your horse's situation by realizing that you're not attempting to touch your toes with someone sitting on your back — someone, by the way, who is not always in balance and harmony!

Since frustration is nevertheless a fact of life in training, it's important to keep finding ways to diminish it. Kelli McMullen Temple, rider of Macavity, the 1989 United States Combined Training Association Horse of the Year, handles frustration by intellectualizing things. She advises riders to evaluate whatever happens on a given day. What was good? What was bad? Then she suggests you formulate a plan to do it better the next day. Accept the idea that getting angry never helps. Remain detached by staying analytical and acknowledging that some days simply will be better than others.

Part of dealing with frustration might involve schooling a horse you don't like. Kelli offers the following advice: "Consider the fact that you only *think* you don't like him because he's not easy for you to ride. If he were easy for you, you'd enjoy him. Perhaps he doesn't understand, is afraid, or physically can't yet do what you're asking. You mustn't take these things personally. The horse is not doing it *to* you. And it's not that you don't like *him* after all. It's that you don't like what he's doing (or not doing). It's unfair to assume that what one horse can easily understand and do will be easy for all."

Your Mental View

Nothing succeeds like success. To train from a positive point of view, hang on to your successes and play them over and over in your mind. (Playing your failures over and over programs you to repeat them.)

How well we ride is often proportionate to our confidence level. So when you're mentally in a slump, replay your greatest success down to the very last detail. Perhaps you'll remember the time you negotiated a particularly tricky course with style and ease. Or maybe you'll relive winning a class that had as many as 35 entries in it. Or how about the horse that just about everyone gave up on, but you were able to train. Bolster your morale with your past successes and you're bound to ride better now.

Use this concept in your daily schooling. Let's say you tend to stiffen a little in canter departs. Since your horse mirrors your body, he too stiffens. Think of one occasion where you've had a smooth depart on that horse. Or on a different horse. Find one memory of a fluid transition and play that over and over in your mind. Do this both off the horse as well as just before you actually canter. If you've never had a good transition, watch someone else and get his execution of the perfect depart planted firmly in your mind.

I remember sitting in a judge's booth several years ago. Gunnar Ostergaard, 1975 Danish National Dressage Champion, came around

When the author pictured the way Gunnar Ostergaard's back looked during his walk-to-canter transition, her own horse did the most lovely transitions, too

the corner. My view had been obstructed until the moment he went from walk to canter. My eye was focused on his back as his horse executed the transition beautifully. For the next three weeks, my horse and I did the most lovely walk-to-canter transitions, as I pictured the way Gunnar's back looked during the depart. Use vicarious experiences as opportunities to create your own successes so that you can break any negative patterns.

Your mental view toward difficulties in training makes all the difference. Not every situation is inherently good or bad. It's the way you choose to see it that determines whether it's positive or not.

Make a game out of seeing the good side of any seemingly bad circumstance. *So you got bucked off your horse yesterday?* Terrific! Now you know you need to spend more time on the longe developing your seat. *You have to miss the first competition of the season because your horse strained a tendon?* Then you're lucky you were given a warning that he has to be made fitter to deal successfully with the demands of the upcoming season. And, once he's rested, you'll have the chance to start a methodical program of conditioning which will bring him to his peak. *Your horse keeps drifting to the right on an approach to a fence?* Take pride in the fact that at least you are educated enough to recognize the problem, and take comfort that awareness is the first step towards improving the situation.

Refuse to see training challenges as a problem. See them as opportunities to make you a better rider. Choosing to see the good in every situation takes effort initially, but eventually it becomes a way of life.

While you are developing this attitude, you might find some little tricks helpful in getting you through the rough spots. For instance, you can detach yourself emotionally by pretending you're training someone else's horse. When you have little at stake personally, it's easier to be patient. If you pretend there is no anxiety, pressure, or deadline, you will not transmit tension to your horse. Consequently, he will probably go better.

Another useful trick is to identify your role in your horse's schooling. Your job as trainer is to find a way to *help* the horse. You don't just make him understand and get stronger. You take him at the point he's been trained to, then you help him to become more of an athlete.

Another positive approach is to deal with the horse as you would deal with a child. Children need discipline and guidelines. In fact, they are more comfortable knowing the limits and what's expected of them than to be left to their own devices. Also, a good parent's demands are based on love rather than anger; discipline is carried out firmly, yet patiently.

It's common for horses to *anticipate*, and this behavior usually has a negative connotation in training. So let's change our point of view towards this as well . When your horse anticipates, appreciate the fact that he is a "tryer," and then find a way to use it to your advantage. The clever trainer uses controlled anticipation to teach. For example, let's say your dressage horse anticipates he's going to halt at X every time he goes down the centerline. Because he anticipates the halt, he stops going forward well before X. So program a new response into him. Teach him to turn down that centerline and extend instead. By getting him to anticipate lengthening rather than stopping, you negate his conditioned response of thinking "halt" (fig. 25).

25   *Because he anticipates the halt, he stops going forward well before X. So program a new response into him: teach him to turn down that centerline and* extend *instead*

Don't get manipulated into saying "no" when a horse anticipates. In order for your training to retain a positive flavor, your concern is not with what shouldn't be done, but with what can be done instead. For instance, you have asked for a canter from a trot each time you cross the centerline. Soon your eager partner anticipates the transition and runs into the canter as soon as he sees that centerline. You pull on the reins and essentially say "no" with your aids. Try substituting a "let's do this instead" for your "no." "How about trot . . . now let's leg yield for a couple of steps . . . now let's lengthen and shorten for a few strides." When he no longer anticipates, "*Now* we can canter."

Your Nature

Part of emotional control comes from understanding and acknowledging your own nature. Then, when it is to your advantage, you can modify your behavior to facilitate training.

The aggressive trainer/rider often needs to learn that less is more. It's not always the one who works hardest and longest, or is the strongest, who is the best. Because horses are by nature sensitive, often the more you do, the more they react negatively. Consider the "cinchy" horse. You tighten the girth and he blows up against it. By the same token, if you use a death grip with your legs on your horse's sides to ask him to go forward, he might swell up against you like the cinchy horse and be less forward. Or by using too strong a hand, your horse comes against you rather than accepting the hand. If you know that your tendency is to be aggressive, and you are having difficulty with certain movements, try doing *less* and see what happens.

Recently while doing a canter half-pass, I wanted to cover more ground sideways. Being physically strong, my first instinct was to drive more. My horse reacted by showing some minor resistance and really did not cover any more ground. So I turned and asked him again by just *thinking* sideways, and we flowed over easily and smoothly. The use of strength had actually blocked my horse's ability to go sideways. Once again I had been shown that less is more. You'd think I'd have totally absorbed that concept by now. But more often than I'd like to admit, my horses have to remind me.

Jane Ashley, dressage judge and FEI-level rider and trainer — also an aggressive, physically strong individual — makes the same discovery again and again. Once while longeing her horse she kept asking him in a loud voice to canter. He repeatedly stiffened and picked up the wrong lead or just ran faster in the trot. Jane then decided to whisper her commands. He calmly responded to what she asked.

On the other hand, the passive or timid trainer/rider can be victimized by the horse. This rider makes few decisions and takes too long to execute them. As a result, he inadvertently "trains" the horse by his absence of direction. For example, every step that you allow your horse to take behind the leg essentially tells him it's okay to not be forward. You must realize and decide that he is behind you and take immediate steps to remedy the situation. Even if you are not effective, you're still telling your horse that what he's doing is unacceptable. And occasionally you'll make the wrong decision as to *how* to correct him. But at least you are training yourself to think and react more quickly. Eventually, the feedback you receive from your horse will give you the chance to learn what you should have done. You can't learn from your mistakes if you don't dare to make some.

Physical Control

In the preceding section we've discussed facets of emotional control while training. Before you can train a horse, however, you must also be in control of yourself physically.

Controlling yourself physically means that you have an *independent seat*. You can use your leg without causing involuntary arm movement. You can use one hand without the other. You can hold your position erect and quiet without tension. You are strong—not strong in the sense of using harsh aids, but physically disciplined to control your body. A quiet body allows the horse to feel refined aids. A body that is banging around out of control forces the horse to filter through all the chaos and shouting to "hear" your signals (fig. 26). Either that or, in an effort for self-preservation, he tunes everything out and becomes dull. Developing control over your position ensures that you won't be the kind of trainer who cries wolf. This happens when your horse gets so used to feeling meaningless signals that when you finally do something relevant, he doesn't believe you.

A body in a technically correct position is profoundly more effective. If two riders apply the exact same aids, the one sitting correctly will have the better influence and results.

One of the best ways to learn how to control your position is on the longe line. Someone else controls the horse so you can concentrate fully on your own body. Since you have no reins, you are unable to find your balance by hanging on your horse's mouth.

When schooling, use the time while your horse is resting to correct

26   *A body that is banging around out of control forces the horse to filter through all the chaos and shouting to 'hear' your signals*

your position. Rest for your horse does not have to be unproductive for you. Use those opportunities when little is going on to perfect your position. As a result, you'll be that much more effective when a lot is going on.

It takes time to develop a habit. That goes for a good habit as well as a bad habit. If you have a problem with your position, devote total concentration to this part of your body for awhile. Perhaps your left leg is always further forward than your right. With conscientious discipline in correcting this fault, your new leg position eventually becomes automatic.

Find exercises that put you in the correct position so you can take advantage of creative imagination and muscle memory. Do the exercise, and then *imagine what it feels like* to do that exercise. For instance, if you have a tendency to sit with one shoulder leading, you can square yourself by reaching back to touch the horse's hip. Then as you ride, *imagine* reaching back to touch the hip in order to make the correction.

Or perhaps you habitually slouch in the air over fences. Do the following exercise. Trot around in a two-point (jumping) position with one arm behind your back pushing an arch into it. Jump in that position once or twice. Then *imagine* that feeling as you jump without your hand behind your back (figs. 27a and b).

27   *If you habitually slouch in the air over fences, jump once or twice with one arm behind your back. . . .*

. . . Then <u>imagine</u> that feeling as you jump without your hand behind your back

Remember, your horse will be in harmony with the way you sit even if that harmony manifests itself as discord. For example, if you come through a corner leading with your inner shoulder, your horse will lean on his inner shoulder. So if you're always complaining that your horse is crooked and carries his haunches to the left, look first to your own position. Is your right leg pushing him over? Is your left hip forward, allowing his left leg to step wide? If you are sure that your position is not creating the problem, then you can assume the horse's leg is weak and proceed to practicing exercises to strengthen his left hind leg.

Positive Mental Training

People "become" the way we see them. Their behavior adjusts to fulfill our expectations. Once, in an elementary school classroom, the teacher was told that one-third of her students were well above average intelligence, one-third were average, and one-third were below average intelligence. The class was divided into three separate groups, and she was told which level of students was in each. She treated them accordingly. She nurtured and encouraged the "brilliant" students and they excelled — eagerly absorbing advanced work. She had little confidence in the abilities of the "slow" students, and they struggled — barely able to satisfactorily complete even minimum requirements. And the "average" students were wholly unremarkable. They neither excelled nor failed. All three groups totally fulfilled the teacher's expectations — despite the fact that, unbeknownst to her, the categories were totally random!

This study points out that not only do we treat people in accordance with the way we see them, but also, as a result of our behavior, they fulfill our expectations of how they will perform. This phenomenon applies to horses as well. So be sure you don't start from a false premise, as the elementary school teacher did in the example above. If you incorrectly perceive that your horse is a "jerk" or a "pig," you will probably treat him roughly or impatiently. He, in turn, will fulfill your expectations and act out a negative behavior. For instance, if you expect your horse to blow up at shows, you will act accordingly and he will react just as you anticipated. Or, if you expect him to bolt when dogs run by, he'll feel your tension and willingly comply. Consider instead that inappropriate actions might be symptoms of misunderstanding, tension, youthful exuberance, or lack of strength — and you might not be so quick to respond to him in a negative way.

I once watched Herbert Rehbein, world-renowned dressage trainer at Grönwohldhof in Germany, do piaffe on an unfamiliar horse who had a history of exploding during this movement. The horse's owner was dumbfounded that the horse had not gone crazy. Rehbein's response was simply, "Horses never go crazy with me — I have tranquilizers in my hands." Because he *expects* them to be calm and obedient, they are.

"Horses never go crazy with me; I have tranquilizers in my hands" — Herbert Rehbein

Of course, if your horse comes to you with a history of negative behavior, it might take some time to change his habitual responses. Until you've had the chance to develop some trust and communication, you should avoid situations that provoke the disobediences. As your relationship grows, carefully begin to ask him to face situations that previously evoked a negative response from him. For instance, if you take your new horse out for a trail ride and suddenly he wheels and tries to run back to the barn, then work in the ring until you've established some trust and communication. Depending on the horse and his history, this could take from as little as several days to as long as several weeks. Once he is confident and obedient in the ring, go out on the trails again, accompanied by another horse and rider. Once he feels secure and enjoys his outings, then ask him to go alone. You'll begin to see your horse as being fun on a hack, now that you've taken the time to help him overcome bad habits.

I remember watching Robert Dover run through a Grand Prix test several days before a show with the volatile Waltzertakt. Every movement was rewarded with a hearty "Good boy!" I asked Robert if he had a particularly nice ride and he explained that by starting to encourage and to praise lavishly the week before a show, he helps the horse to feel confident and good about himself. The horse perceives that he is wonderful and obedient, and this becomes a self-fulfilling prophecy at the competition.

For Robert, mental training of the horse has resulted in the submission of some very exuberant and headstrong characters — like Walzertakt and Federleicht. He is quick to differentiate, however, between submission and subservience. Submission is a positive force. You essentially make a deal with the horse by which both of you have the same goals and interests. Your horse feels confident and he understands your requirements, so he actually wants to do what you ask. Subservience, on the other hand, is *forced* submission. The rider dominates the horse in a tyrannical way. This takes away the horse's desire to achieve, of his own volition, the required goal. As a result, he does what you demand mechanically — without expression.

To train from a positive point of view, it is advantageous to ride in *maintenance* rather than *correction*. It must be demoralizing for the horse to constantly be told, "No, that's wrong." So, be aware of the things that your horse does habitually and make an effort to maintain what you have (forward, straight, regular rhythm, acceptance of the bit) rather than allowing these qualities to degenerate, and then having to fix or correct them constantly. For example, if your horse is in self-carriage, maintain this balance with subtle half-halts rather than letting him fall on the forehand and then having to make a strong correction. Or keep your horse straight between your legs and hands as you approach a fence, so that you don't have to correct him for wavering. If you're the kind of rider who makes too many corrections, see how long you can go purely in maintenance. Can you make it all the way around the arena in quiet harmony? You might be surprised that you can do 50% less than you thought.

Schooling and developing a relationship with your horse is exciting and rewarding. Let your training be your showcase. Every day provides you with a fresh opportunity.

Have a standard of perfection in your mind. Then take the pressure off yourself by realizing you will never reach perfection. But revel in striving for excellence. The journey is just as fulfilling as the destination.

Robert Dover

Part Three

COMPETITION

Winning is one's own pursuit of individual excellence.
— D. Waitley

COMPETING should be an adventure. It can be a healthy outlet and a rewarding experience for both you and your horse. Having a goal to work towards enhances training. After all, to accomplish something, you must *plan* to accomplish something.

The planning stages leading up to competition can also make you aware of gaps in your horse's training. Let's say you've decided that your horse's stage of training is appropriate for competing at Second Level in dressage. By working towards competing in a specific test, you might discover a weakness in his lengthenings. Then you'll need to improve his suppleness, strength, and balance in order to develop those lengthenings. Or perhaps in the course of advancing from Novice to Training in eventing, you find that the increased cross-country speed (from 350 meters per minute for Novice to 400mpm or 450mpm for Training) causes your horse to hesitate, jump in bad form, or stop altogether. Therefore, when schooling, you'll have to work at gradually increasing the speed until your horse can cope with the difficulty of going faster. Or if, in show jumping, you find that when you move up from 3' courses to 3'6", your horse is losing form over the fences. Maybe he hangs his knees or hollows his back or drags his hind legs. You'll need to strengthen your horse by schooling over gymnastic lines at both the trot and canter. You can also practice riding whole courses at home — gradually increasing the height of the fences and working on the same distances you would get at the shows.

Without the deadline of a specific competition, it would be easy to ignore what is difficult and concentrate just on what is easy. Unfortunately, the most difficult things are usually what your horse needs to practice the most.

Don't be discouraged by the discovery of these weak areas. Instead, appreciate your growing awareness. How exciting! Now you can start a systematic program for improvement. Besides developing the horse through such a focus, working towards your goal and meeting the deadline also gives you a tremendous feeling of accomplishment.

But don't get bogged down by perfectionism either. It's unrealistic to decide that you'll make your debut only when you can win. Instead, do your homework and get out there for the exposure, the experience, and the fun. Use your performance and the judge's comments as measures of your progress. Set goals that are challenging, but not impossible.

Above all, don't let fear of failure prevent you from getting out there. It is better to do something and fail than to do nothing at all.

8

Preparation

The very nature of competition involves stress. You have to deal with variables that you don't encounter when schooling on a daily basis. You're not on your home territory. You're riding in front of a judge. There are other competitors and spectators watching. You have to be ready at a certain time. You must ride prescribed movements or perform at a given moment—not when you feel best prepared.

Preparation is the key to handling these variables effectively and making competition a positive experience. Thoughtful preparation will allow you to control the things that *can* be controlled, since there will always be some factors—like the weather and the footing—that are out of your hands. The better prepared you are, both mentally and physically, the less you'll be overwhelmed by various stresses. The stresses will still exist, but their adverse effects will be minimized. Stress can actually add to the excitement and exhilaration. How boring life would be without some degree of stress. Thorough preparation, however, will help you keep stress at a manageable level.

The Dressage Test

Homework begins several weeks before competition. It's vital that you are totally familiar with the dressage arenas and the tests. This will enable you to *ride your horse rather than ride the test*. You should be able to go through the test on automatic pilot so that you reserve all your concentration for feeling what your horse is doing.

The final score for your test reflects the combination of artistic and technical aspects. You will not earn high marks for riding a beautifully moving horse while executing an inaccurate test. Nor will you be rewarded for a precise test performed on a horse that is stiff and tense. Good scores are awarded to the horse who best exemplifies the qualities listed in the judge's marks for general impressions—not just who performs a technically correct test. These collective marks reward the horse whose paces are free and regular, who moves freely forward with a supple back and engaged hindquarters, who accepts the bridle, and who is attentive to and in harmony with the rider.

In order to ride a technically correct test, you must have a clear understanding of the movements you are performing, and, of course, have your horse enough on the aids so you can execute the movement. To begin, let's get as comfortable in the arena as you are in your own living room. There are two sizes of arenas, small and standard. The small arena measures 20 x 40 meters while the standard arena measures 20 x 60 meters. If you're used to riding to X in the small arena for your 20-meter circles, you'll have to switch gears in your mind when working in the large arena. Otherwise, your 20-meter circles will turn out to be 30-meter eggs! Many of the Training Level tests are done in the small arena. However, it is important to check your program when you arrive at the showgrounds. Just because Training Level, Test 1 is in a small arena does not necessarily mean that Training Level, Test 2 will be as well.

Both arenas are divided in half lengthwise by the center line. Each of these halves is again divided lengthwise by the quarter lines. Since the arena is 20 meters wide, each of the sections is 5 meters wide. The two quarter lines are 10 meters apart. The center line is 10 meters from either long side. Each quarter line is 5 meters from one long side and 15 meters from the other long side (diagram VI).

In *both* sizes of arenas, the letters M, F, H, and K are 6 meters from the corners. Many novice riders think that they are 10 meters from the corners, and therefore use them erroneously as a reference point for a 20-meter circle. As a result, their circles aren't round. It is also useful to remember that the other letters on the long sides of the *standard* arena (P,B,R,V,E,S,) are twice that distance apart — 12 meters. In the *small* arena, however, the remaining letters (B and E) are 20 meters from the corner or 14 meters from the corner letters (diagram VII a, b, c).

The dimensions of both arenas must become second nature to you. Educate your eye to see distances. Get out in the arena on foot. Stand on the center line and visualize 5 meters to the quarter line. Then pace it off to check and train yourself. For instance, your score for 15-meter circles will be influenced by how accurately you hit those quarter lines. Technically, the directive remarks on the score sheet for a circle also include the size and shape of the circle. (The size is 15 meters while the shape should be completely round without any bulges or flat sides.) If you overshoot or undershoot the quarter line on a 15-meter circle, you will lower your score regardless of how well your horse is going. But a smaller circle is less of a fault than a larger circle. A too-large circle makes it appear that the horse cannot cope with the increased engagement of the smaller required figure; he therefore makes it larger to avoid the difficulty of the movement. So,

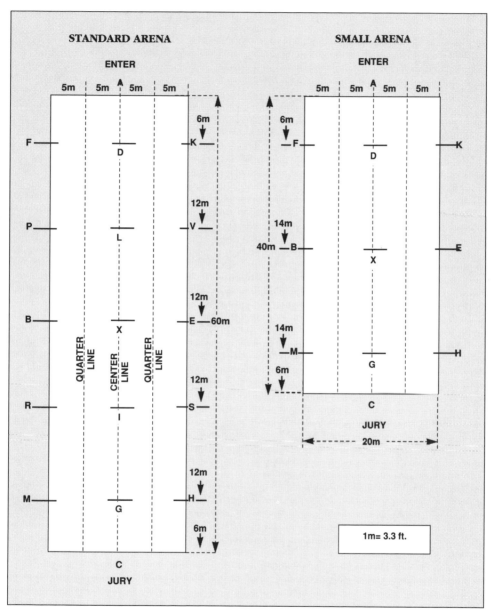

Diagram VI. Arenas for dressage competitions

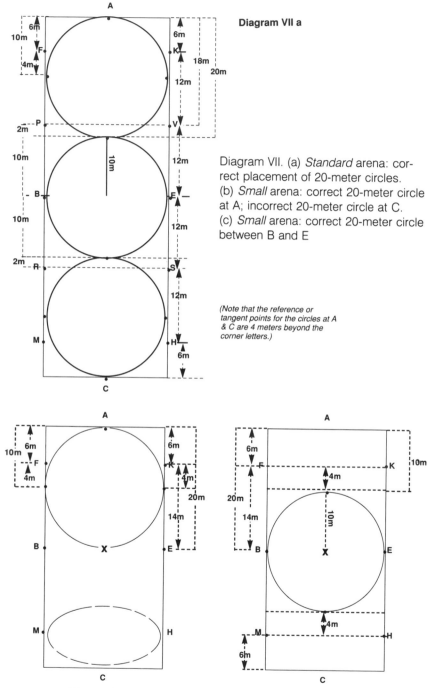

Diagram VII a

Diagram VII. (a) *Standard* arena: correct placement of 20-meter circles. (b) *Small* arena: correct 20-meter circle at A; incorrect 20-meter circle at C. (c) *Small* arena: correct 20-meter circle between B and E

(Note that the reference or tangent points for the circles at A & C are 4 meters beyond the corner letters.)

Diagram VII b

Diagram VII c

what is in actuality a rider error is *also* perceived and penalized as the horse's lack of flexibility and balance.

Once you are familiar with the dimensions of the arena and the placement of the letters, analyze the figures and movements you are asked to perform for each test. Diagram these figures on paper. Walk them out on foot. Know exactly where you will begin your turn on and off center lines in order to do a smooth arc. Plan well ahead so that you do your transitions when your body is exactly at the letter. Go through the test mentally so that you know where the difficult parts will be and can plan what to do about them. Having done all this homework, you'll be able to be accurate with little conscious effort by the time you actually ride.

Sue Shirland, Grand Prix dressage rider who coaches nationally-successful young riders, advises the novice to learn tests with one's own personal directions. Write your test out or obtain an official score sheet that has blank spaces after each movement (reserved for judges' comments). Go over the test movement by movement and write down the personal instructions that your trainer might give you. Let's say you've turned across the school at B and you're approaching a right turn at E. On your sheet, write down "At X get the bend, make sure he's on the left rein, give him a half-halt." Your directions can include reminders about your position: "Inside shoulder back here" or "outside leg back in the turn." Sue believes that this kind of preparation is especially helpful when circumstances limit the actual amount of riding time you have to prepare for a particular test.

For instance, you don't have sufficient time to prepare because your horse has an injury. Since you have to ride conservatively as he returns to work, you can avoid a lot of wear and tear by analyzing your tests on paper rather than drilling on horseback.

Or perhaps you're the one who can't work. I found this approach enormously helpful when I was preparing for the AHSA National Finals in Culpeper, Virginia, in 1987. I planned to show Jolicoeur in the Fourth Level Freestyle and Prix St. Georges, but I was sidelined ten days before the competition with a torn intercostal muscle (the muscle between the ribs). In an effort to alleviate the pain, the doctor injected the muscle with cortisone. Unfortunately, the needle went in too far, punctured the pleura (membrane) surrounding my lungs, and one of them collapsed. I found myself lying in a hospital bed unable to ride. I still planned to compete, but despaired over not being able to practice. So, I dissected my tests, wrote down my personal directions, and rehearsed daily in my imagination. Despite the fact that I was quite weak and surely not riding my best, I went through the rides on autopilot thanks to my passive preparations. In the end, Jolicoeur and I went on to win the Freestyle Championships and we were fourth in the Prix St. Georges.

Memorizing Dressage Tests and Jumping Courses

Do whatever you can to eliminate the stress of worrying that you may forget your dressage test or jumping course. You can have someone read the test aloud to you at dressage shows, but riders have been known to make errors even while having the test read. If you opt for a reader, plan to know your test anyhow and use the reader as a back-up in case you forget something. Learning jumping courses is a bit different from learning a dressage test because the courses vary from class to class or event to event. But basically you can use the same techniques.

You can learn your dressage test or jumping course through a variety of approaches:

> a. Verbal
>
> b. Physical
>
> c. Diagrammatic
>
> d. Psychocybernetic

Use any or all of these four techniques.

a. To learn a dressage test verbally, memorize it *completely* so that you can not only recite the test from beginning to end, but also start anywhere in the body of the test and know the movements before and after. Get to the point where you feel like you're popping in a tape cassette of a particular ride, and the pattern of the test flows out. I've found this particularly effective when I've had to memorize a lot of different tests. If I draw a blank while in the arena, I can just say "Second Level, Test 2" and the pattern appears clearly in my mind.

Do the same thing with your stadium and cross-country courses. Recite it from beginning to end (e.g., liverpool to brush box to red and white vertical to one-stride combination) and then mentally select any single jump and recall which fence comes before and after.

b. Physically, you can practice your dressage test both on and off the horse. If your living-room rug is conveniently rectangular, you can do the test on foot at home. While riding, practice either segments or the whole test frequently so that it really flows.

As for jumping a cross-country course, unless you know the terrain really well, walking the course three times is optimum. On your first walk, go with a trainer, an accomplished rider, or a friend you can bounce ideas off. Keep in mind or even jot down the instructions that your coach recommends (for instance, balance when you make that turn by the stone so that you can ride forward the last three strides, or shorten the horse's stride for that bounce but keep the energy). On your second walk, become familiar with the terrain. Know the approaches to the jumps. Give yourself reference points or landmarks where you'll make striding, pace, or position adjustments. On your third walk, you should walk the course exactly as you will ride it. Use your landmarks and rehearse in your mind the particular adjustments you'll make. Your walk should flow just as your ride will.

Walk your stadium course twice. The first time go with a coach or follow a rider you respect. On this walk, learn the pattern of the course and the technical aspects, such as how your horse's length of stride relates to the combinations. Walk the course the second time exactly as you will ride it. Make sure you walk out all your corners and utilize your space as you will when mounted. Know how the distance in the lines and combinations will work for your horse so you can decide *when* to lengthen or package his stride.

c. It's helpful to diagram dressage tests so that if you verbally draw a blank, you can conjure up a mental picture of what comes next. See the diagram of Training Level, Test 2 (diagram VIII). By using different colors or symbols to designate the three gaits, you can tell at a glance where you should be in the arena and what you should be doing. This technique is particularly useful for those who are visually oriented. Diagrams are also convenient for refreshing your memory just before you ride.

You're provided with a map for cross-country, so take it along when you walk the course and make notes on it. Write down landmarks or special points to remember.

Sketch your stadium course as well but do it as a pattern (long side/diagonal/long side) rather than as individual fences (diagram IX).

d. Perhaps the most useful technique for memorizing dressage tests and jumping courses is to apply psychocybernetic principles. Let us quickly review the basic concepts:

- Your subconscious mind consists, in part, of a goal-striving mechanism. It is impersonal and will do its best to accomplish whatever goal you put in front of it (success or failure).

- Your subconscious can not differentiate between what is real and what is imagined. The more frequently you imagine the "perfect" ride, the more your mind believes you've actually done it. You can therefore program yourself for success.

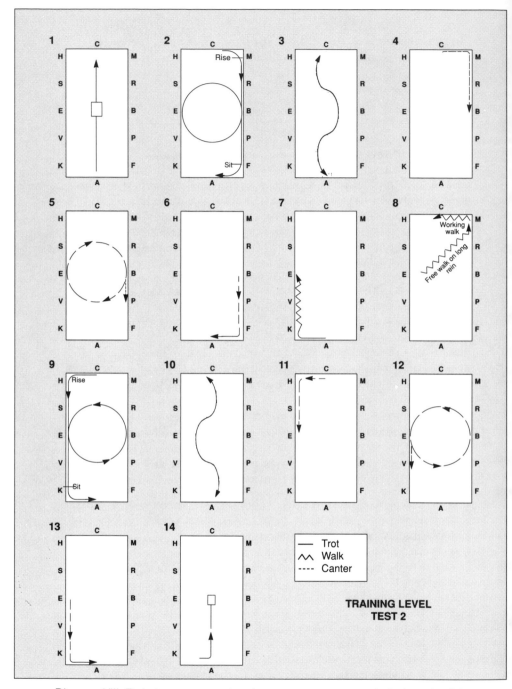

Diagram VIII. To help you memorize dressage tests, use symbols (or colors) to represent different segments

- The more vividly you imagine, the better. Use all your senses. See the white tape on the braids, feel the lace on the reins, smell the fresh spring air, hear the sound of your horse's breathing.

Practicing in your imagination is a powerful tool. You can create your own "movie magic," producing and directing down to the very last detail. In your movie ignore the fact that during the canter depart at M, your horse usually stiffens. Instead, see the perfect transition — fluid, forward, and on the bit. In cross-country, edit out the part where your horse hesitates on approaches to a water jump. Instead, see him jumping into the water eagerly and confidently. For stadium, your movie version disregards your horse drifting towards the out-gate and instead shows him cantering on easily to the next fence.

Have fun with your movie. Try different camera angles (fig. 28). Use an overhead camera. See the ride from the judge's perspective or from behind the horse. Visualize the perfect ride from the saddle, or watch yourself as if you were on a movie screen. Use whatever approach allows you to fill in the details most vividly. With practice you'll become more and more adept at filling in those details. If you

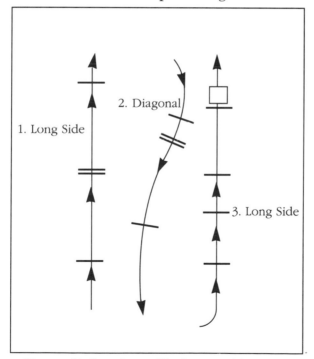

Diagram IX. If you have difficulty memorizing your stadium course, visualize the whole pattern such as long side/diagonal/long side

can imagine yourself flying (without a plane, remember?), you can also visualize the perfect ride. So see every stride, every corner, and every transition executed gracefully and flawlessly. Complete every course with style and ease. Experience your state of relaxation and the harmony between you and your partner. If things begin to fall apart during your actual ride, hold steadfastly to your perfect movie-image. You can't change what has already happened, but you can get back on track, without being rattled, by continuing to ride *as if* everything were going smoothly.

Start the psychocybernetic filmmaking a few weeks before your show and "screen" your perfect ride at least once a day. For dressage, do the tests you'll be riding at the show. For jumping, create an imaginary course or reride one from the past. The best time to "watch" your movie is when you are most relaxed. Set aside some quiet time during the day, or perhaps wait until bedtime just before you drift off to sleep.

Further Use of Psychocybernetics in Competition

Since your performance is often determined by your warm-up, bring your visualization skills to the warm-up area. If you've practiced imaging during training, you'll have developed the skill and concentration level necessary to shut out distractions. Distractions such as other horses and riders, unfamiliar surroundings, or substandard footing become incidental when you stay focused on the task at hand.

Use your imagery skills to shut out distractions even further. When in a frenetic or disturbing atmosphere, narrow your focal point down to include the image of just you and your horse. Try making yourself and your horse appear quite large and the people watching rather tiny. Or make the image of you and your horse crystal clear, while the people watching are dim and out of focus. Since they are too small or blurry for you to see who they are, you won't be concerned about what they might be thinking. Kim Walnes, Bronze Medalist at the 1982 Three Day World Championships, takes this concept one step further. Kim says, "I create a vacuum around me and my horse—a space where only we exist and where I create any atmosphere I want. On a sluggish horse I build a sense of electricity. On a nervous horse I imagine riding in the security of my own backyard."

Kim is a great believer in the power and influence of the imagination. She tells the story of a horse she had to train who would not enter the jumping area at a show, although he was quiet at home. "He would rear and spin with great agility, always getting farther away.

28 *Have fun with your movie. Try different camera angles*

Conventional methods of breaking the habit weren't working, so at his next competition, I concentrated all through the warm-up on images of him being at home, staying calm, and trusting me. As our time to go drew nearer, I played the image over and over of him calmly cantering in, halting for the salute and proceeding in a forward manner. When our turn came, I held the image firmly in place, and he cantered in quietly. There was a half-stride hesitation a few steps in, but I never let the image falter, and on he went to complete a course at a show for the first time!"

I never cease to be amazed and delighted by the results I achieve by programming my mind with vivid mental images. In 1990, during Genaldon's first season at Prix St. Georges and Intermediare I, we were consistently making mistakes in the lines of flying changes of lead every second, third, or fourth stride of the canter. I had less than a week between my last competition and the Olympic Festival selection trials (Tampa, Florida, April 1990) to sort this situation out. So each day I would visualize line after line of mistake-free changes. I would see the whole picture — myself sitting on Genaldon riding

"I create a vacuum around me and my horse, a space where only we exist and where I create any atmosphere I want" — Kim Walnes

diagonal after diagonal of clean changes. Occasionally I would shift the emphasis of the picture. Sometimes I would focus on my horse executing the changes, while other times I would see and feel myself giving the aids correctly and in a relaxed way. This was important to do because the repeated mistakes had created anxiety and tension in both of us, which in turn caused more mistakes. The images helped me break the undesirable cycle. Sure enough, during the competition we executed all lines of changes for the first time ever with no mistakes!

Practice imaging daily, but never engage in negative rehearsal. Or as Grand Prix dressage rider Kathy Connolly says, "Never allow yourself to think 'What if?'." It's counterproductive to rehearse "*What if* my horse shies at the judge's box?" or "*What if* my horse loses his footing on the slippery approach to the water jump?" That kind of practice causes the very thing you want to avoid. So if you find yourself getting caught up in negative rehearsal, do some thought-stopping to nip that kind of practice in the bud (see p. 51).

Rehearsal

In addition to rehearsing in your imagination, you can, in reality, rehearse in a variety of ways with your horse. Do some dress rehearsals at home before you go to your first show. Wearing your coat and hat, ride a dressage test with someone sitting at C standing in as the judge—they don't have to be critiquing you. Or rehearse a mock stadium course. Put on your show clothes and, with your horse, go through the motions of jumping a course right down to saluting the judge, waiting for the bell, and cantering your initial circle before you go through the start flags. This trial run will help you to feel more prepared; as a result, you'll be more confident.

The exact duration of a good dressage warm-up is difficult to gauge. You might allow 30 minutes and discover too late that you needed 45 minutes. Plan for this by rehearsing tests at home with only a minimal warm-up. Your practice ride might not be brilliant, but at least you'll know that you can get through it.

Olympic veteran Lendon Gray feels that the novice can help overcome show nerves by rehearsing at home in front of lots of people. "Part of those nerves comes from wondering 'What are people at the show going to think of me?' If you feel that way, one thing you can do at home is to grab anyone and everyone to sit and watch you until it's not a big deal anymore." In the privacy of your own barn you can learn to eliminate the distraction of riding in front of others.

Regarding equipment, try to avoid using anything brand new — such as a saddle or boots — without first practicing at home with them. Even if you've bought new saddle pads for show, rehearse with them at least once before the competition to see how they feel. You have enough to contend with without having to adjust to the unfamiliar sensations of new tack and equipment.

Consider factors like weather and footing in your rehearsals. If you normally ride first thing in the morning when it is cool, you might be in for a nasty shock if all your rides are between noon and three in the afternoon. Your horse needs to acclimatize to heat and humidity in the same way you do. If it's pouring one day, make a point of riding in the rain to see how he deals with rain and deep footing. If you usually ride on sand, you might need to get the feel of your horse on grass before you head off to the local show. He might behave or react very differently; but now you won't be disconcerted by what you are prepared for. You might even decide to have him shod with rim shoes or shoes with holes so that you can use studs in case the footing is slippery. How disappointing to have to ride conservative lengthenings just because conditions are such that you'll slide eight feet on the downward transitions. Or receive time penalties on cross-country because your horse did not feel sure-footed.

Prepare, prepare, prepare. The more prepared you are before you ever set foot on the showgrounds, the more enjoyable your experience will be. But despite all your best intentions, some things will still go wrong in competition. What do you do then? Prepare some more! Work out potential problems by doing coping rehearsals while you are still securely at home. Imagine all the things that might go wrong, and then visualize successful resolutions to your problems.

For rehearsing how to cope with unexpected behavior, the big question is always, "What do I do *when?*" With the help of a qualified coach, one can learn how to answer those "whens." *When* my horse starts moving at the halt, I will ride forward to make it look like it was my idea to move off, rather than having an argument over standing still. *When* my horse picks up the wrong lead, rather than canter all the way around I will quietly bring him back to the trot, reorganize, and ask for the canter again. *When* my horse feels like he's going to run out to the right at the coop, I will drop back behind the motion with my upper body, use an opening left rein, and keep my right hand close to the withers. Knowing "what do I do *when*" is comforting because all your decisions have been made ahead of time. As a novice it's virtually impossible to make decisions effectively while showing. That takes experience and exposure. With experience, you'll be able to evaluate as you go. But until you've logged those competition miles, you should have every imaginable scenario prepared for in advance with a positive plan of action.

One of the ways to overcome those nasty surprises in the dressage arena is to rehearse your tests from *start to finish* at home. No matter what happens, correct the mistakes and *continue*. Don't repeat the movement. If your horse breaks in an extension or misses a flying change, don't circle back and ride the movement again. Instead, carry on and complete the test as if it were the real thing. This will give you invaluable experience at home, developing the poise to get back on track after you've made a mistake.

Plan all your rehearsal so that you feel prepared at least a week before the actual show. Then relax and ride your horse without pressure during that final week. Frantically drilling in the last days before a show just increases tension. Perhaps you'll simply do confidence-building work that last week, without tackling any huge fences or difficult movements. And, if you've been having serious confrontations with your horse, make your peace during the final days and enter the competition as friends.

Carry this feeling with you to the show. The show is not the place to school your horse. You are not going to "fix" your flying changes the day of your competition. Do your schooling at home and live with whatever you have.

Reducing Tension

People and horses function optimally when relaxed. Yet competition lends itself to an atmosphere of tension and arousal. You need a plan to foster relaxation so that you and your horse can produce peak performance.

Prior to competition, spend time practicing the skills of deep breathing, progressive relaxation, and autogenic relaxation discussed earlier. Begin well ahead of show season so that by the time the first competition rolls around, you will be adept at using these relaxation techniques. Then, when you're feeling tense at a show, you can always fall back on these skills.

For example, one competitor used deep breathing (p. 18) to overcome the panic she felt about forgetting the dressage test during her ride. She knew that her tension was being simultaneously transferred to her sensitive thoroughbred with disastrous results. Typically, she'd start to relax only about halfway through her ride; she noticed that her scores were always better towards the end. She overcame this pattern by imaging the perfect ride at home and writing down her own personal directions for the test. Then, when it came to the actual ride, she performed the test on autopilot, concentrating on deep breathing for the first few minutes. Once she herself had settled down, she could shift her focus to her horse. As a result, her scores were consistently better through the entire test and her personal enjoyment improved dramatically.

You can also use progressive relaxation (p. 18) to become extremely relaxed—quickly and at will. When you first get on your horse, mentally search around your body for specific parts with tension. Your experience with progressive relaxation should make it easy for you to identify tight muscles. If your neck feels tight, contract it even further, let the tension build for five seconds, then let go. Follow by taking a deep breath. Evaluate your body for any other residual tension. If you find it, tense and relax that area again.

If you prefer, take advantage of autogenic relaxation (p. 20). While warming up your horse, take a deep breath, exhale, and say the words "I am calm" to yourself. Do this several times. Your body has already been programmed to react to those words if you've done your homework with autogenics. The words will gently encourage you to let go of your tension.

Another way of reducing tension is to plan at the beginning of the season to compete at a level that is lower than the one that you are schooling at home. You are at the competition to show and be evaluated on what is established. It's very difficult to feel confident at a level on which the work is not confirmed. You have so many other stresses to deal with in competition—why add to the pressure? Compete at a lower level so you can relax and have a good time.

9

It's Showtime!

Arrive Early

Arrive at the showgrounds in plenty of time so that you don't feel hurried and frazzled. I have actually known riders who deliberately did not allow sufficient time. Who could blame them, then, for putting in a lousy performance? After all, they only had a seven-minute warm-up! They obviously came to the show already equipped with their handy loser's limp.

If either you or your horse needs the extra time to relax, be kind to yourself and enjoy the luxury of arriving the day before. That way you can ride around the grounds (at least once) and allow yourself and your horse to settle in and adjust to the new surroundings without any pressure. Take your horse for a walk, put him away; then do it again a couple of hours later. Both of you will be more relaxed by the time you have to compete. Remember, this is not the time to be schooling your horse. Let him just relax and settle in.

Arriving early at an event gives you the chance to get the lay of the land. After settling your horse into his stall, pick up your packet — which contains your program, pinney for cross-country, bridle number for dressage and stadium, and cross-country map. Find out where the dressage and show jumping phases will be held. Organize your tack. You'll be less nervous if your equipment is thoughtfully laid out. And be sure to reorganize after each phase for the same reason. You can also write out a schedule that looks something like this:

8:00 — Tack up for dressage

8:20 — Mount up

8:50 — Ride dressage test

10:30 — Walk cross-country course three times

1:00 — Tack up for cross-country

1:20 — Warm-up for cross-country

1:45 — Cross-country start
2:30 — Groom horse
3:00 — Walk stadium
3:45 — Tack up for stadium
4:15 (approx.) — Ride stadium

Arriving the day before gives you a chance to check out the arena and inspect the footing. If the arena is open, enter it and go through your test on your own two feet. *Without your horse*, walk, trot, canter, and do the school figures so that you'll feel familiar with the arena. Even though the dimensions of arenas are always the same, each one has its own feel. Having done this, you'll feel like you've already ridden there once by the time you actually compete. The newness will be gone, and you won't be surprised, say, by the deep footing in the corner by M, or by the section of the grass arena where one of your lengthenings will be slightly downhill. Be sure not to take your horse into the arena unless the organizer has allowed it, since you could be eliminated.

Most likely the arena will be closed. If that's the case, stand at A and repeatedly visualize yourself and your horse performing your entire test gracefully and accurately.

This is also the time to decide on the most strategic way to get a straight entry into the arena down the center line. Is there sufficient room to circle outside the end of the ring, or do you need to ride parallel to the long side and then arc onto the center line (diagram Xa)? If there is room to circle, be sure to do it to the left or right of the center line. That way, when the bell rings you can maintain the same track and simply continue down the center line (diagram Xb). You risk losing the balance you've established, or missing the center line altogether, if you make a large circle and then have to cut it in half (diagram Xc).

If your horse is a straight mover, it's a good idea to plan riding your circle in the same direction as your turn will be when you get to C. (This helps jog your memory as to which way to go at C). However, if your horse is a crooked mover, you might want to try a different starting strategy. For instance, if he tends to travel with his quarters to the right, circle in whichever direction gives you greater control of the haunches. This way, you will have a much better chance of riding a good, straight entry down the center line.

As for the cross-country phase—which you must walk on foot— take advantage of arriving early by walking the course several times

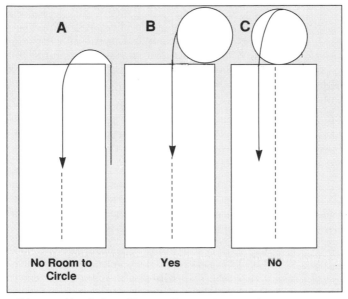

Diagram X a, b & c. Choose the most strategic way to get a straight entry down the centerline

(see p. 116). Allow plenty of time for these course-walks and familiarize yourself really well with the terrain. Don't be surprised if you occasionally get lost walking a course the first time. Usually there is some helpful person also walking to guide you back on track. Then make sure you go back and rewalk the correct route!

The stadium course is not always open at the beginning of a horse trials. If there is no "course open" sign, check with show management. When you organize your schedule, plan a time for doing your stadium course-walk. Depending on your cross-country times and when the course is open, it may be either before or after cross-country.

Observe Other Riders

Getting to the showgrounds early also gives you the opportunity to watch other riders practicing. It's helpful to concentrate on the good horses and riders and to fix their images firmly in your mind. Observe not only their positions and styles of riding but also their confidence and poise. Watching bad riders might hold some kind of negative fascination but it's not going to help your riding and could possibly hurt it. If you do watch bad riders, be clear that your objective is to learn from their mistakes—realizing what you must *not* do in any given situation. Seeing *what not to do* can be beneficial to your own learning process. But in my personal opinion, the danger of focusing on bad riders is that it provides negative images. This could actually drag down your own performance by subconsciously programming the mistakes into your mind. That's why I advise just watching the riders you want to emulate. Study the experts. If you wanted to be a dancer, you'd pattern yourself after the best there is. If you wanted to make a lot of money, you wouldn't take fiscal advice from your neighbor who is broke. Watch only those who have been successful doing what you want to do.

Observing others is educational, but it may be risky when it comes to the other riders competing in your own dressage class. It can be unnerving to watch your fellow competitors when you haven't ridden yet. Suddenly all the horses and riders look like Olympic Gold Medalists Reiner Klimke on Ahlerich—while *you're* having a problem keeping your right foot in the iron! So when you're about to compete, put your blinders on and focus totally on yourself.

Of course you should take advantage of watching well-respected riders in your jumping classes—it's both instructive and inspirational. Watch different horses and riders jumping in order to see what works. Watch rhythm and sequence, and how the course is riding. Once you get the idea of the flow, don't watch if it makes you nervous. For cross-country, watch good riders negotiating tricky portions of the course. But *don't* change your plan if you feel you have the right one for your horse. Realize that these riders are riding their own horses who have their own quirks; they therefore might require a different approach than your horse.

Warm-up

Allowing sufficient time for warm-up is critical. You'll have to do a bit of planning here. Know where you'll compete, the best route to get there, and where you'll warm up. Once you've determined what time you want to start your warm-up, work backwards to plan your preparations. In your calculations, consider whether or not you'll have a helper, since he or she can save you a lot of time and energy. Include plenty of time for grooming, going over your test or memorizing your course, retaping a braid, and adjusting tack. You don't want to be forced to cut short your actual warm-up time. By the time you mount, you should feel unhurried and in control.

Planning the warm-up itself is probably the most variable factor in your show preparations. It can change from competition to competition, ride to ride, and horse to horse. Even weather is a consideration. You'll probably need extra time to warm up on a cold, blustery day in order to take the edge off your horse. But on a hot, humid day plan a short warm-up or else your horse will be wilted by the time you compete. As you become more experienced and more familiar with your horse at shows, it gets easier to plan warm-up times. Until you reach this point, it's probably better to err on the side of too much time. If you feel your horse is ready, you can always walk him around until it's your time to go.

It's helpful to have a routine in warm-up. All the other horses and people who tend to be in warm-up areas can be distracting. A specific routine serves as a soother and pacifier. Know exactly what you're going to do and stick to it no matter what. Don't be intimidated or influenced by what others are doing. Stay with your tried-and-true program because it'll be easier to become focused if you have no unexpected decisions to make.

Set up your routine beforehand with your instructor, if you have one. For example, let's say you are planning to ride a specific dressage test—First Level, Test 4. This preparation might take a total of 40 minutes in good weather. Use the first ten minutes to walk on a long rein. During the next five to ten minutes, trot and canter long and low to loosen up. Then start to organize your horse. Ride transitions within the gait (lengthenings and shortenings) in trot and canter as well as from gait to gait. Take a short break. Then work on your 10-meter circles and begin your leg-yields. Plan to be finished warming up five minutes ahead of your scheduled start time so that you can put on your jacket, wipe your boots off, or make any other last-minute preparations.

If you are competing at a horse trials, perhaps you'll plan a 20-to-30 minute warm-up for cross-country (including time to hack over to the start). If your horse is feeling full of himself due to the excitement of going cross-country, get up into your galloping position and canter quietly around until he settles into a nice rhythm. Or find another quiet spot to do your initial warm-up (such as a dressage arena that is not being used). Once the horse has settled somewhat, do some short lengthenings in trot and canter in both directions to make sure he is easily adjustable. Then to get started, jump a cross-rail from the trot. Next, canter a vertical fence to an oxer. Then perhaps jump the oxer a couple more times at cross-country speed. Adopt an aggressive, determined cross-country state of mind to inspire your horse during the warm-up. If you aren't feeling confident and bold, act "as if" you are.

In your warm-up for the stadium phase, remember that your horse might be stiff after cross-country — so allow a good ten minutes for a quiet walk at the beginning. Your program should include being able to shorten and lengthen your horse's stride. You want to be sure he's still not in his cross-country galloping stride. If he feels strong, you might take a couple more practice jumps than you did when you warmed him up for cross-country. Remember, your goal in stadium is to *not* knock the fences down. So be sure you have your horse soft, balanced, and ridable to the jumps.

With your warm-up completed, you're ready to compete. Don't get uptight if your legs feel like spaghetti. Just relax and enjoy yourself. Have faith that all your preparations — rehearsal, imaging, relaxation — will enable you to have an outstanding ride.

Sue Shirland believes that often the major difference between who wins and who comes in second boils down to attitude

10

Attitude

Develop a Winning Attitude

In competition, as in most everything, your attitude determines how far you can go. Grand Prix dressage rider Sue Shirland points out that often the major difference between who wins and who comes in second boils down to attitude. To illustrate her point, she recalls the 'Battle of the Brians' during the 1988 Winter Olympic Games. Brian Boitano from the United States and Brian Orser from Canada were the top contenders in men's figure skating. According to Sue, "They were equally talented and equally prepared to go for the gold. Jump for jump they were evenly matched. They both had fabulous costumes, music, and choreography. Each spent countless hours perfecting their skills. On any given day it should have been up for grabs who was gonna win.

"But you knew going in who would capture the gold. You could tell from the interviews. Brian Orser appeared distressed by his past losses. He seemed negative and subdued. On the other hand, Brian Boitano was up, psyched, and really looking forward to the competition. The outcome was a foregone conclusion."

You might not be Olympians like 'the Brians,' but your attitude plays just as great a role in your own level of competition. You should therefore consciously develop attitudes toward competition that enhance your performance.

Let's discuss some of the things you'll have to contend with at shows. Competing, itself, is a personal thing. No one else's opinion or performance matters. Strive for your personal peak performance.

You are going out and showing what you and your horse have achieved together in training. It's a partnership. You love your horse. He trusts you. And you're proud and excited to be here together. If you adopt this attitude, you'll be less concerned about what others think and more able to enjoy and revel in your accomplishments. The personal satisfaction is enormous.

In your mind, change your role from a defensive one. Turn the tables. Don't think in terms of being critiqued by judges, trainers, or spectators. Indeed, if it suits your personality, get yourself psyched up by riding for the audience. Help the spectator to enjoy the beauty and creativity of two living creatures working in harmony. Ride for those who are watching and who want to see you shine and you can in turn use that energy from the crowd to heighten your performance.

Find words that appeal to you and try to capture their essence. Convey the feeling of "elegance," "polished," or perhaps "joyful."

If you're riding dressage, change your attitude towards the judge. He is not this frightening being who is ready and eager to destroy you. Most good judges *want* to award a perfect score of 10. So greet the judge warmly as you circle outside the arena. As you come down that center line, look him squarely in the eye and say to yourself, "I'm very proud to be riding for you today."

Show-Nerves

When faced with the initial prospect of competing, don't let fear stop you from setting your goal and working towards it. Fear comes in many forms — fear of failure, fear of looking foolish, fear of falling off your horse. To win, you must be willing to take a risk. And so what if you blow it. A year, six months, even one month from now, it really won't matter and will be mostly forgotten. Each time you make a mistake, consider it part of your education: learn from it and try again. It's the persistence, the trying again, that will eventually enable you to overcome your anxiety and achieve your goals.

Understand that action cures fear. Inaction feeds fear. The longer you procrastinate, the larger that mental monster grows. Jump right in and do whatever has to be done! You'll find that your fears shrink.

You'll also derive enormous personal satisfaction from controlling your fears, rather than allowing them to control you. Dealing with your fear is courageous. I have a student who is relaxed at dressage competitions but terrified when she rides in events. I was puzzled as to why she would put herself through this ordeal. One day I asked her why she kept on eventing if she was so afraid. Her answer was simply that her tremendous feeling of accomplishment made it all worthwhile.

You can also overcome your show-nerves by — believe it or not — lying to yourself! Actually, you are just using the power of positive speech. At first you really tell yourself that something you are feeling (such as fear) simply isn't so — but with repetition, this "lie" eventually becomes a reality.

For example, years ago I used to "lie" by telling everyone that I loved to compete. I repeated these lies over a period of time until, in fact, they were so programmed into my mind that I truly came to love competing and rarely felt nervous. It was exciting to *choose* the way I wanted to feel and then program myself to become that way through the power of positive speech.

One of my students used to get paralyzed with tension when it was time for her to enter the dressage arena. I had her "lie" in order to help her with her problem. We rehearsed with a judge's bell. Every time I rang the bell she would lie aloud by saying, "Oh, goody! It's my turn! I can't wait another second." At first, what she said sounded so absurd that she would giggle to herself—and that alone helped to break up some tension. Eventually, the power of positive speech took over and she reached a point where she did indeed feel eager and excited to get in that arena and show what she could do. This approach is a lot more positive than hearing a judge's bell and saying to yourself, "Oh, God! I'm not ready . . . I need a few more minutes . . . I hope he doesn't shy at the flowers by A . . . Here goes nothing."

Grand Prix dressage rider Kathy Connolly believes "you can handle show-nerves by having a program for success. Success is a learned behavior. Success is a habit. It comes down to concentration and focus. Teach yourself an unshakable concentration mode where there is no other option and no margin. At a show, everyone is concentrating. The winners concentrate on what it takes to do well. Those who don't do well are also concentrating. But they are concentrating on things that will hurt their performance."

Kathy goes on to say that you can handle the pressure of showing "by first learning to identify the thought patterns that create a negative psyche. Then control it by replacing the negative thoughts with positive ones. You might need a little help from a coach or friend or sports psychologist to identify when the negative pattern starts. What are the trigger points that begin to undermine your self-confidence? Do you become too particular and perfectionistic at home a couple of weeks before the show? Are you panicked because your spouse or an owner or some other person who makes you nervous is watching?

"The general answer to all these questions is: The most important person for you to do well for is *yourself*. You must refuse to be held back from your goal by anyone, especially yourself. Do not become self-denigrating. These are all normal feelings and you must find ways to calm yourself. Fear is something you allow to happen to yourself. You are completely responsible for what you have in your mind. So focus on desired results."

Kathy has helped a lot of riders deal with their show-nerves

"Never allow yourself to think 'what if?'" — Kathy Connelly

through various thought-stopping techniques (see p. 51). She says "Sometimes it's sufficient to say to yourself 'Cancel, cancel' when the negative process begins. If that is not enough, try unrelated words like 'chocolate ice cream cone.' Or wear an elastic band around your wrist and give yourself a sharp twang with it to get out of a negative mind-set.

"Next you must learn to project and visualize what you want. Project a feeling of serenity and calmness. Then visualize you and your horse doing what you want beautifully."

Remember, there are no "what ifs?" Don't obsess about what *might* happen, because you'll soon find that your fixation creates conditions that will make it happen. Stay in the here and now. After all, that's all there is.

Stay Positive

Don't reduce yourself to the level of the pessimistic competitor by complaining about the horrible conditions. It might be true that it's too hot, too windy, too rainy or that the footing is too deep, hard like concrete, or uneven. Just remember, that everyone has to ride in the same conditions — that is the great leveler. If you refuse to complain, and therefore repel the negatives from your mind, you will rise above everyone else's stumbling blocks. To go one step further, you can take comfort in the thought that the bad weather and footing will most probably distract some of the *other* riders. That in itself will give you an advantage, since you've already refused to give the problems more than a passing thought.

Often I hear people complain about their position in the starting order. This is where the power of words can psych you out. The most common complaints I hear are, "I'm the first rider of the day" or "I'm the first rider in my class." Also, "I'm in the same class with Ms. Hotsy-Totsy-Professional, so what chance do I have?"

If you're the first rider of the day, and you fear that the the judges are "cold" and don't have their scoring perspective yet, concentrate instead on how fortunate you are to be riding when it's the coolest time of day and the warm-up areas are fairly deserted.

If you're first to go in a class later in the day, comfort yourself with the fact that it's *not* the very first ride of the day and the judge by now has his perspective.

If you ride following an excellent horse and rider, decide that this will ensure your success. Think positively! When that rider is finished, the judge will be in a great mood. Then you come in and ride such a *fabulous* test that your scores have to be even higher!

Rationalizing? Sure. But what difference does it make as long as you enter that arena full of confidence. All these rationalizations are helpful in keeping your attitude intact and preserving your self-confidence. Now you can wholeheartedly pursue *your* peak performance.

Winning and Losing

Part of your enjoyment of competition will be determined by your attitude towards winning and losing. It's easy to be excited when you bring home the blue ribbon. What you need to be able to do is look at losing with the right perspective. As Shakespeare's Hamlet said, " . . . there is nothing either good or bad but thinking makes it so."

Winning is all in the way you look at it. I remember my friend Fredda, an amateur dressage rider, being tremendously excited when she had placed seventh in a very large class at a dressage show in Florida. I was happy for her but a bit perplexed, because when I went to the scoreboard, I discovered that I, not Fredda, was seventh in that same class. When I asked her how that could be, she replied, "Oh, Jane, you don't understand. You count from the top while I count from the bottom!" Fredda was sincerely thrilled that there were six riders *below* her.

You can "win" by bettering yourself personally each time you are in the arena. That way you can feel satisfied with both yourself and your performance, rather than your actual placing in the competition. According to Zig Ziglar, "Doing your best is more important than being the best."[1] And psychologist Denis Waitley says, "Winning is coming in fourth exhausted and encouraged because last time you came in fifth."[2]

As far as losing is concerned, Thomas Edison had the right perception. Rather than seeing himself as having failed 10,000 times while working on an invention, he declared that he had *successfully* found 10,000 ways that did not work! So, don't despair when your horse is tense or perhaps tired in your dressage test because you pressured him in warm-up or you warmed up too long. And don't worry that you totally missed the striding in that eight-stride line because your horse was behind your legs or that you knocked down three fences because you didn't warm-up long enough and your horse was too strong. Get excited! Now you'll know to avoid those mistakes in the future.

It's important to remember that it doesn't matter how many times you stumble and fall, but how many times you get up. The common thread that runs throughout the philosophy of winners, when it comes to losing, is to learn from their mistakes. Failure is part of the learning process necessary for achieving anything worthwhile. [3] *Learn* from your failures. Listen to the comments from the judges or your trainer, then go home and do your homework.

It's okay to feel frustrated and disappointed with yourself at the time you lose. That feeling is not merely a luxury — it's a necessity. Otherwise you'll redirect the negative feelings and they'll come out in other undesirable ways. So feel frustrated for five or ten minutes, and then develop the cosmic perspective on losing: Look at the planets and recognize how insignificant we are and how unimportant this competition really is in the big picture.

Keep this psychocybernetic principle in mind: Errors, failures, or embarrassments are important in the learning process. They are a means to an end. When they have served their purpose, forget them! Because if you dwell on them in your imagination, the error becomes the goal. [4]

Success is measured in many ways besides a blue ribbon. Grand Prix dressage rider Nancy Smith, U.S. Equestrian Team Bronze Medalist at the 1989 North American Championships in Canada on Felit, tells her students that winning is just being able to ride in competition as well as you do at home. It's also being able to think and make choices. Whether or not you make the right choices or can execute your strategy is beside the point. With time and experience, you'll be more effective. The important thing is that you are thinking.

Nancy also advises the novice to keep success in perspective by not taking the judge's score out of context. The judge is evaluating from an ideal, from a 10 down — while you are coming from a zero up. Let's say you get a score of 4 for your right-lead canter because your horse broke once. A 4 is considered an "insufficient" score. But suppose that the last time out, you couldn't even get him to pick up the right lead at all. For you, that 4 is an improvement and a positive accomplishment.

It's important not to compare the scores from one judge to another or from one show to another. Although the marks should be universal, the nature of judging is subjective. So your 58% from Judge A in First Level, Test 1 might, in fact, have been a better ride than your 63% from Judge B in First Level, Test 2. Your score sheets are informative, but they don't tell the whole story. Consider the judge's *comments* to be the more accurate reflection of your performance, and be sure to keep the actual score in perspective.

Event rider Kelli McMullen Temple has a healthy perspective on winning and losing. Recently she has had tremendous success with her horse Macavity at the highest level of Three Day Eventing. Kelli's reaction to all the excitement surrounding her victories is that " . . . the ribbons are the icing on the cake. It's the day-to-day training that I love. And although it's nice to be rewarded with public recognition, I'm doing the same things and having just as much fun as I've had for the last ten years. Besides, when all the shouting is over, you still have to drive home. You have your horses to ride the next day. You still have to go to the grocery store."

On the occasions when she loses, Kelli keeps things in the same wholesome perspective by reminding herself that it's only one event. She looks for the good things that came out of it. She realizes that she'll live through any disappointment, and that there's always another event coming up.

Another way to assess your accomplishments beyond simple winning or losing is to reflect on your 'firsts'. "This was my first Three Day Event." Or, "This is my first time competing at an A-rated horse show." Your 'firsts' are strictly between you and your horse. It's fun to celebrate these occasions.

After the performance, you can always feel victorious about your personal milestones. Perhaps this was the first show where your horse didn't buck at the canter depart. Or, it was the first time you completed cross-country with no jumping faults and no time penalties. Or maybe this is the first competition where you didn't feel nauseated before your ride. Even if the overall performance was not up to your expectations, you can always come away with a positive feeling of winning if you make an effort to search for these special milestones.

So set your goals, acquire the necessary knowledge and skills, have a plan, carry out your thorough preparations, and make sure your attitude is properly adjusted. Then get out there and do it! Don't let anyone — least of all yourself — dictate any limits. The joys of competition with your partner are to be fully experienced and savored.

FOOTNOTES

Introduction

1. "The Winner's Edge." Audio tape by Dr. Denis Waitley. (*Listen & Learn USA*)

Chapter 1

2. *The American Heritage Dictionary*
3. "The Winner's Edge"
4. *The Miracle Man* by Morris Goodman. Prentice-Hall, 1985, pp. 44-5
5. *See You at the Top* by Zig Ziglar. Pelican Publishing Co., 1978, p. 294
6. "Getting Help from the Head Doctor" by Dr. Robert Rotella. (*Practical Horseman, May 1988*)
7. "The Winner's Edge"
8. *The Psychology of Winning* by Dr. Denis Waitley. Berkley Books, 1979, p. 71
9. *Psycho-Cybernetics* by Maxwell Maltz, M.D. Pocket Books, 1960, p. xii
10. *See You at the Top*, p. 192
11. *The Psychology of Winning*, p. 125
12. From a taped conversation with Dr. John McCauley, May 1989

Chapter 2

1. *Seeds of Greatness* by Dr. Denis Waitley. Pocket Books, 1983, p. 21
2. "The Winner's Edge"

Chapter 3

1. *Psycho-Cybernetics*, p. 68
2. *See You at the Top*, p. 136
3. *The Psychology of Winning*, p. 5
4. Ibid., p. 5
5. Ibid., p. 77

Chapter 4

1. *See You at the Top*, p. 188
2. Ibid., p. 63
3. Ibid., p. 108
4. *Success Through a Positive Mental Attitude* by Napoleon Hill and W. Clement Stone. Pocket Books, 1977, back cover
5. *See You at the Top*, p. 320
6. Ibid., p. 33
7. *The Magic of Thinking Big* by J. Schwartz. Prentice-Hall, 1965, p. 24

Chapter 5

1. *1990-91 AHSA Rule Book*. The American Horse Shows Association, Inc., 1989, p. 133

Chapter 10

1. *See You at the Top*, p. 332
2. *The Psychology of Winning*, p. 9
3. *The Miracle Man*, p. 137
4. *Psycho-Cybernetics,* p. 66

PHOTO CREDITS

Frontispiece	Terri Miller		65	V. J. Zabek
Page	13	Mary Phelps	83	Mary Phelps
	30	Stacy Holmes (above)	97	Mary Phelps (above)
	36	Susan Sexton		Susan Sexton (below)
	39	Kit Houghton	105	Susan Sexton
	57	Photo Czerny (above)	107	Fred Newman
	60	Susan Sexton	122	Gower Photos
	61	Mary Phelps	132	Terri Miller
	63	Susan Sexton	136	Susan Sexton

Index

Age, 61-62
Aids, as punishment, 75-79
Arena, dimension of, 112-115
Ashley, Jane, 29, 31, 100
As If Principle, 38-45, 86
  desirable personal qualities
      and, 40-45
  and psychocybernetics, 38-39
  and show-nerves, 39-40
Attitude
  in competition, 138
  positive, 46-48
  winning, 133-134
Autogenic relaxation, 20-22, *see
      also* Relaxation exercises

Bannister, Roger, 46
Behavior modification
  of horse, 68-81
  of rider, 100-101
Belief, 12-14
Bliss, Nancy, 56, 57
Boitano, Brian, 133
Breathing, diaphragmatic, 18

Commitment, 11
Competition, 110
  arriving early for, 127-129
  imaging and, 120-123
  levels of, 90
  observing others in, 129-130
  preparation for, 111-126
  rehearsal for, 123-125
  tension reduction in, 125-126
  warm-up in, 130-132
*Complete Training of Horse and
      Rider,* (Podhajsky), 72

Confidence, 44-45
Connelly, Kathy, 123, 135-137
Coolidge, Calvin, 12
Courage, 41-43
Criticism, dealing with, 54-55

Davidson, Bruce, 43, 45
Diaphragmatic breathing, 18
Discipline, 45
Disobedience, 68, 74-79
  vs. resistance, 87
Double Win, (Waitley), 39
Dover, Robert, 12, 35, 36, 106
Dreams, 10
Dressage test
  memorizing, 116-120
  preparation for, 111-115

Edison, Thomas, 138
Emotional control, 94-101
Emotional involvement, 27
Enthusiasm, 40-41
Exercises
  relaxation, 18-22
  visualization, 22-25

Finances, 64-66
Fredda, 138
Frustration, 94-96

Goals, 5-7
  negative, 7-8
Goal-striving mechanism, 2-4
Goodrich, Pamela, 59-60, 69
Gray, Lendon, 62, 63, 123

Hamlin, Jane, 65, 66
Horse
    resistance by, 87-94
    shortcomings of, 62-64
Horse in front of the leg, behavior modification in training, 79

Imaging, 15-17, 18-25, 120-123, *see also* Visualization
Imaginary experience, *see* Imaging
Inspiration, sources of, 54

John, 46-48
Jumping course, memorizing, 116-120

Legs, in behavior modification, 68-73
Leng, Virginia, 39, 86
Ljungquist, Bengt, viii, 72
Loser's limp, 56-66
Losing, attitude toward, 138-140
Luck, 9

Maltz, Maxwell, 2, 4, 35, 48
Matz, Michael, 86
Maria L., 43
McCauley, Dr. John, 18-22
Mental images, *see* Imaging
Mental view, positive, 96-100, 104-107, *see also* Positive attitude
Movements, analyzing, 72-73

Negative reinforcement, *see* Punishment, Reinforcement
Negativity, eliminating, 48-50
Nesmeth, Major, 15
Nightengale, Earl, 40

Oerter, Al, xii
Orser, Brian, 133
Ostergaard, Gunnar, 96-98
Otto-Crepin, Margit, 83

Patience, 43-44
Persistence, 12
Personal qualities, desirable, 40-45
Physical disability, 56-59
Podhajsky, Alois, 72
Poise, 44
Positive attitude, 46-48, 85-86, 137-138, *see also* Mental view, positive
Positive reinforcement, *see* Reinforcement, Reward
Practical Dressage Manual (Ljungquist), 72
Progressive relaxation, 18-20, *see also* Relaxation exercises
Psychocybernetics, 2
    and *As If* Principle, 38-39
    and memorizing competitive activity, 117-120
    and WIN mechanism, 82-85
Psycho-Cybernetics (Maltz), 2
Psychology of Winning, (Waitley), 30, 41
Punishment, in behavior modification, 68, 74-79

Rehbein, Herbert, 105
Rehearsal, for competition, 123-125
Reinforcement, in behavior modification, 68, 73-79
Reins, in behavior modification, 68-73
Relaxation exercises, 18-22
Resistance, by horse, 87-94
Response, in behavior modification, 68

Reward, in behavior modification, 68, 73-74
Rotella, Robert, 8
Roycroft, Bill, 62

Saltonstall, Tacie, 47, 64
Sangdahl, Jean, 62
Savoie, Jane, ii, 4, 8, 12-13, 36-37, 39-40, 50, 64, 66, 83, 100, 115, 122-123, 135
Seat, in behavior modification, 69-73
Self-control, physical, 101-104
Self-image, 48
Self-talk, positive, 35, 85-86, see also Words, power of
Shirland, Sue, 115, 132, 133
Show-nerves, 134-137
  and As If Principle, 39-40
Smith, Nancy, 139
Stevenson, Nini, 59
Stevenson, Wendy, 59
Stimulus, in behavior modification, 68-71
Stuckelberger, Christine, 86
Sydnor, Cindy, 33, 37, 55

Temple, Kelli McMullen, 13-14, 95-96, 140
Tension, reducing, 125-126
Thought-stopping, 50-52

Time, management of, 64

Uphoff, Nicole, 61-62

Visualization, 22-25, see also Imaging

Walking the course, 116-117
Walnes, Kim, 86, 120-122
Waitley, Denis, 39, 41, 109, 138
Warm-up, in competition, 130-132
Will, strength of, 59-60
WIN mechanism, 2-4, 27, 82-86
  belief and, 12-14
  commitment and, 11
  dreams in, 10
  goals in, 5-8
  luck in, 9
  persistence and, 12
  psychocybernetics and, 82-85
  work and, 11
Winner's Edge, (Waitley), 39
Winning, attitude toward, 138-140
Words, power of, 28-34, 36-37, see also Self-talk, positive
Work, and WIN mechanism, 11
Worry, eliminating, 52

Ziglar, Zig, xiii, 138